COURAGE

FOR THE FORWARD PATH

**Wisdom and
Stories**
from 30 Years of
the Journey in
Christ

from Journey Canada

Courage for the Forward Path
Copyright © 2021 by Journey Canada

Tellwell Talent
www.tellwell.ca

ISBN
978-0-2288-6779-1 (Hardcover)
978-0-2288-6778-4 (Paperback)
978-0-2288-6780-7 (eBook)

Table of Contents

First Steps, Brancaster

This is the day to leave the dark behind you
Take the adventure, step beyond the hearth,
Shake off at last the shackles that confined you,
And find the courage for the forward path.
You yearned for freedom through the long night watches,
The day has come and you are free to choose,
Now is your time and season.
Companioned still by your familiar crutches,
And leaning on the props you hope to lose,
You step outside and widen your horizon.

After the dimly burning wick of winter
That seemed to dull and darken everything
The April sun shines clear beyond your shelter
And clean as sight itself. The reed-birds sing,
As heaven reaches down to touch the earth
And circle her, revealing everywhere
A lovely, longed-for blue.
Breathe deep and be renewed by every breath,
Kinned to the keen east wind and cleansing air,
As though the blue itself were blowing through you.

You keep the coastal path where edge meets edge,
The sea and salt marsh touching in North Norfolk,
Reed cutters cuttings, patterned in the sedge,
Open and ease the way that you will walk,
Unbroken reeds still wave their feathered fronds
Through which you glimpse the long line of the sea
And hear its healing voice.
Tentative steps begin to break your bonds,
You push on through the pain that sets you free,
Towards the day when broken bones rejoice

-Malcolm Guite, *The Singing Bowl*

Preface

In early 2021, I was invited to a meeting of the 30th Anniversary Committee of Journey Canada. The committee had a serious challenge—how to mark what God had done through the ministry since 1991, including engaging everyone who had been involved since its inception, while in the midst of the uncertainty and stress of a global pandemic. Traditional events like banquets, retreats, and seminars were obviously no-gos and everyone, EVERYONE was thoroughly, truly, and deeply sick of looking at each other on computer screens. What to do?

At the first couple of meetings, the committee kicked around several ideas. I had a little concept in the back of my mind regarding a Journey book, but I was a bit hesitant to mention it. I thought perhaps the idea was too ambitious, too unoriginal (a lot of ministries write a book to mark an anniversary), or too nerdy. But mostly, I was worried it would be *too much work*.

Nevertheless, I put the idea of a book forward, thinking no one would take it seriously. After all, I had no idea how to write a book. What I had not counted on was that no one else on the committee had written a book (although Toni Dolfo-Smith had collaborated on some academic books in his earlier career) and they all knew that I was the communications guy, so they naturally believed I could pull it off.

A couple of ideas came out of the meeting that made the project seem feasible. The most important was that it wouldn't be a single-writer thing—we would ask people from all across the ministry, throughout its history, to contribute. The other idea was that this would not be a straight history of the ministry, but rather a book that talked about Journey's approach to spirituality—a book that would encourage and edify. We wanted something anyone could pick up to find wisdom.

There is no question that this book would not have come together without the help and support of Kirsten Rumary and Toni Dolfo-Smith, who served on the editorial committee with me. They provided great insights and feedback and Toni championed the book in a way that got people involved and excited. I'd also like to thank Arabella Cheng, Bruce Mills and Rosemary Flaaten from the Journey 30th anniversary committee for their help in making this a reality, and Elinor Hanschke who worked on the book's production.

The result is a devotional book from a variety of voices. Editing this book, working with these writers, and reading their insights has been a huge privilege. My prayer is that it encourages you just a fraction as much as it has encouraged me.

Graeme Lauber
Calgary, 2021

Introduction

by the Editors

The editors are Toni Dolfo-Smith, Kirsten Rumary, and Graeme Lauber.

Toni Smith arrived in Vancouver at the end of the 1980s with two goals—to get married and to get a degree that was just for himself and not to impress his father. He enrolled in a seminary program at Regent College and, more importantly, married Mardi Dolfo in 1989.

In his first year at Regent, Toni found himself being approached by fellow students, many of whom were desperate, struggling, and anxious about their relationships and sexuality. These men began to gather in Regent's atrium for times of sharing and prayer, with Toni offering leadership. By the end of the year, Toni felt that he was out of ideas and resources for leading the group. Fortunately, it was about this time that he met Leanne Payne.

The 1990s—A Ministry is Born (and Begins to Grow)
Through Payne, Toni and Mardi discovered resources and friends to help them further develop the work they were doing. They discovered the material being used by Living Waters in the United States and from Payne they learned some of the techniques that were important in prayer ministry. So, in 1991, drawing on these things plus their own ministry experience and reading, the Dolfo-Smiths were able to offer the first ever program in Vancouver. At this time the ministry was called *Wellspring*. In these early days, Barbara Pain became a key voice as she saw the importance of the

ministry and the way that God was calling Toni to pursue the work, even when he did not always see it.

For the first few years, the courses were a simple, once-a-week side project that took place while Toni and Mardi were pursuing other priorities, including education, careers, and a family. But the mid 1990s saw a shift—the ministry hosted its first conference in Vancouver in 1994, hosted by Eric Stephanson and the University Chapel. 1995 saw the first international training event at Harrison Hot Springs in BC's Fraser Valley. In fact, the mid-1990s saw a unique outpouring of the Spirit all across Canada. The most obvious expression of this was the Toronto Blessing, which began in 1994 (and caused no small amount of controversy among Christians). Much of what was happening with Living Waters/Journey at that time was a part of this work of God. The training events from the mid to late 90s were unique and powerful times of healing, both spiritual and physical, and times of rapid growth for the ministry.

While there were connections between the work of Living Waters in Canada and the ministry of the same name in the US, the Canadian work remained distinct. Over the course of the 90s, a number of people committed themselves to building the work and provided a uniquely Canadian flavour. This showed up in a strong culture of teamwork, and one of the signs of that was the team effort involved a few years later when the Canadian Manual was written and developed.

By 1996 some of the structures around the ministry were beginning to formalize. There was a board, led by Eric Stephanson with Barbara Pain, Tim and Sarah MacIntosh, and Steve and Christina Stewart as members. It was also about this time that Toni began to take a small stipend to work for the ministry one day a week. In 1993 the Vancouver ministry began to work with other ministries across Canada in centres like Calgary, Edmonton, Winnipeg, and Montreal (in 1995), where others had begun to look into healing prayer ministry. Toni also began to travel to Europe to support the ministry there. In 2000 Journey launched its internship program with Kirsten Rumary as the inaugural intern.

The 2000s—The Teen Years

2001 was not only the year that Journey celebrated its tenth anniversary, it was also the year that Toni started to work for the ministry full-time and made his first trips to Asia. The following years were ones of growth—staff was added, bigger offices were found, the internship program went international, and a new manual was written. By 2011, the Journey ministry had taken on an international flair and Toni began working with Lisa Guinness and Ron Brookman to build the global ministry with resources and overall leadership provided by the Canadian work.

The early 2000s were not all positive. Canada legalized same-sex marriage in 2005 and the church in Canada responded in odd ways. The legal change could have been a good opportunity to reflect on the theology of sexuality and why the church believed and taught as it did. Indeed, it was a time when God was calling His people to something deeper than mere sexual ethics—to move from behaviour to a true spirituality of intimacy and connection and to a realization that we had not properly understood the body and the role of marriage in God's creational plan for us. Instead, in many ways, the church in Canada chose to hide, preferring to change the subject. Since Journey had a ministry in relationships and sexuality, some of the church connections and opportunities for speaking disappeared.

The 2010s—Potential Disasters bring Maturity Instead

If 1995 had been a seminal year for growth and realizing the work that God wanted to do through the ministry, 2012 was a landmark year for the trials it brought—trials that ultimately led to good things. In February of 2012, on the morning of Ash Wednesday, the staff in the national office gathered for prayer. There was a sense among the group that God was beginning to call Journey into new things, but it was not entirely clear what that might mean. As they prayed, the staff called out to God, "Lord, do whatever you want to do." That night, the national offices of Journey in Vancouver burned to the ground.

The fire was a shocking and, in many ways, devastating event, but it also brought a strong sense that God was doing something new. New office space was found quickly in a location much closer to the center of Vancouver and a Global Conference of the burgeoning international ministry was held just four months later. In the years that followed, Journey also changed its name from Living Waters to Journey, a move that signalled a shift in its approach to ministry with an even deeper focus on Christian spirituality and identity. The leadership structure also advanced, with the board of directors shifting to a governance model and the creation of an executive team, with Daniel Komori as Associate Executive Director and Ricky Lee as Operations Director.

In 2013, a Journey Discipleship Course was infiltrated by a journalist for the first time. A reporter from the Toronto Star entered a course in Ontario under false pretenses and, in an innuendo-filled article, tried to suggest that Journey was involved in so-called "conversion therapy"—the attempt to change people's sexual orientation. The response to the Star article was complex—many people saw the headline and took away a negative impression of the ministry. Those who read the article soon learned that what the journalist had uncovered were some beliefs with which he didn't agree. The comments section on the article expressed so much outrage against it that the Star eventually shut them down. However, the event was simply the first in a string of false accusations that persisted for several years in the media. Journey took several lessons away from this experience: We learned how to respond to the accusations effectively in the media, we learned that cultural attitudes to sexuality had moved very far from the Christian understanding, and we saw that the path we had been on—an increasing focus on identity and relationships—was the correct one.

This last trend was perhaps one of the most important for Journey. The ministry is committed to walking with people who want to experience Jesus in all aspects of their sexuality, and we understand that it becomes a controversial topic, primarily due to the shame that accompanies it. When people were able to talk about the shame that they were experiencing and know that they were still loved, they were able to find freedom and enter into the life that Jesus died to give them. Journey will never compromise on the belief that God has designed sex to be between one man and one woman in marriage, but the ultimate vision is much larger—to see people set free from shame and to enter into whatever Jesus is inviting them to with joy and, perhaps most important, with the love and support of fellow Christians. This is an encompassing vision for Christian spirituality and identity.

Journey's vision of Christian spirituality is not an easy one. It often involves looking at the hurt and pain that we have experienced and taking stock of the ways we have responded to that pain in unhealthy and even sinful ways. It is also a spirituality that is rooted in a deep conviction of the love and mercy of a good God, a compassionate Saviour, and an always-available Spirit. The journey we are on is difficult, but with the help of God and His people, we can find *Courage for the Forward Path.*

Chapter 1

An Invitation to Travel
by Graeme Lauber, Editor

In May of 2015 I stepped onto a plane with my wife and three children to take several flights from Calgary, Canada to Doha, Qatar. Doha is not a major tourist destination and we were not heading there to see the sights—I had accepted a job and we were moving halfway around the world to see how living in the scorching desert of Qatar compared to the frozen prairie of Canada. Doha was going to be our new home.

The first time I left North America was to move my family over 11,000 kilometers to live in Arabia. I like to think this sounds exotic. The truth was that I was finding my life a little stifling, a bit uncomfortable, and I was looking to strike out and find some adventure. I wanted my kids to see a bigger world, and I wanted to see some of it for myself. I've heard Newfoundlanders who said, "you should go outside just to blow the stink of the house off you"—in essence to allow the breeze to freshen up your clothes. I wanted that for my entire life.

So, we set out on a journey, and that journey took us to France and Belgium and India and Jordan. Although we were based in Doha, we travelled regularly. London and Dubai began to feel familiar. These trips were not always comfortable. We had a particularly stressful and difficult time in Sri Lanka as we learned the challenges of travelling in a developing country. But it was so worthwhile, and I loved every minute, despite the discomfort.

In this book, we are using travel as a metaphor for the spiritual life. This analogy seemed sensible in light of the name of the Journey ministry, and it is a common enough metaphor throughout the history of the people of God. Probably the most obvious travel story in Scripture is the one of the Exodus, as the people of Israel leave Egypt to find their way as God's chosen nation in the Promised Land.

The Exodus has some very clear points of comparison with our own spiritual journeys. It took a lot to get the people of Israel pried out of Egypt in the first place. Just getting the journey underway was a huge operation involving frogs, gnats, darkness, blood, and death. Travel means change, and change almost always leads to resistance, both from within our own hearts and from the people around us. Even choosing to set out and begin this voyage can be very difficult.

Nor did things run particularly smoothly once the children of Israel were underway. Many of them complained and wanted to go back to Egypt, and the Egyptians chased them to bring them back. The trip was hard, and the progress agonizingly slow. The relationship between God and Israel was not simply bumpy, it was often out-and-out antagonistic. The people wanted to return to their old ways, and they kept falling into the same idolatrous, comfortable traps over and over. But God was faithful, and they were eventually brought to the promised land.

Even once Israel had arrived at their destination, things were not as they had hoped. There were hostile people already there, and entering into the promises of God was not as easy as simply setting up a few tents. They soon learned that although they had made progress, the problems that had accompanied them through the desert were going to be with them in the new country.

The story of the Exodus can serve as both a comfort and a warning for us in our own spiritual travels. We may think that if we only work on our spirituality for a period of time—a month, a year, a decade—we will eventually achieve some sort of enlightenment and move past struggle, temptation, or the experience of pain. However, no matter how much progress we make in the Christian life, we will never grow beyond our need for the power and grace of Jesus. Just as the people of Israel depended on the faithfulness of God to support them and lead them to where they were going, we are always dependent on Him for our own spiritual sustenance and progress.

And so, there are limitations on our metaphor of the journey, since it can give someone the impression that it is possible to "arrive" in the spiritual life—to come to the place where we have achieved something. The truth of the matter is that progress in the spiritual life is simply progress in understanding how much we need Jesus.

The book that follows is divided into five sections. The first three sections are structured around the three aspects of the Exodus I've outlined above—departing, travelling, and "coming home"—and they reflect the messiness and limitations of the process. The final two sections are about the journey itself: section four concerns itself with the companions sent to accompany us, and the final section is about the road we walk—the path of prayer. Each section has seven chapters, and so you could use this book as a five-week devotional, if you choose.

This book is a compilation of the stories and reflections of people from across Canada and around the world who have had some sort of connection to the ministry of Journey over the years. Throughout the book you'll read different voices and see people with varied concerns and ways of approaching the spiritual life. We have tried to preserve the original voice of each author and our hope is that if you are not able to resonate with every chapter, you will at least find a few chapters that speak to you.

Almost all of the chapters in this book mention the writer's experience with the ministry of Journey Canada. There may be readers who pick this book up, however, and know nothing of the work that we do. Journey Canada is involved in two things. First, we provide the church with help and training in meeting some of the most challenging issues of our day, particularly when it comes to matters of identity, relationships, and sexuality. However, the heart of what we do is provide a safe place for people to talk about their experiences and the things that may have held them in shame and feelings of inadequacy. We want people to experience the love of God and other people as they talk about their lives. And then we pray and we ask God, in Christ Jesus, to speak into each person's situation.

At the centre of what our ministry does is the Journey Discipleship Course (JDC), an 18-week program where men and women worship together and hear teaching on matters pertaining to personal identity. If the JDC is at the heart of the ministry, small group time is at the heart of the JDC. In small groups we are able to share deeply, in a confidential and supportive environment, and then we engage in listening prayer together, hearing what Jesus would want to speak to us.

My decision to move to the Middle East was, in many ways, made possible by my experience at Journey. As I learned to live beyond shame and to trust my own God-given judgement I was able to make bold decisions and stand by them. My metaphorical spiritual journey led to a literal journey.

We have found that allowing people a safe place to be honest, and then to experience love and compassion, can be life-changing. We hope this book will be a part of your own spiritual path.

Section 1—Setting Out

Beginning a journey is almost never easy. There are any number of preparations to make, packing to do, pets to be cared for. Even if we're looking forward to the trip, we know that there will be some discomfort at being away from home—we may have to bunk with someone rather than having a room to ourselves, the beds may be too hard, the food too spicy, we may not be able to find a decent cup of coffee. Some of this is part of the fun, but some of it is why we say there's no place like home.

Setting out on our spiritual journey may not just be inconvenient or uncomfortable—it can be downright painful. It often involves taking stock of our lives, confronting the pain of our past and the reality that we have not always faced that pain in live-giving ways. Most of us would rather stay "at home" spiritually—content to live our lives the way we've always done, even though home is often a broken-down shack. It's at least familiar, if not exactly comfortable. The bleak reality can often be that the pain of staying home has to be greater than the pain of the journey before we are willing to take the first step. This is why few people choose to travel.

The chapters in this section are honest about the difficulty of the spiritual journey on which we're embarking. They articulate the challenge that lies before us—a challenge that, according to Becca Brunner (chapter six), can feel like tearing at our own skin. However, each one sounds the note of hope—pointing to the healing that Jesus offers.

Even as we start out, we already know the end of this journey—healing, freedom and abundant life, offered through Jesus. We can set out filled with hope, because we know where this trip is taking us.

-GL

"Have Mercy on Me" by Andrea Heavenor - Acrylic on Canvas

I wake and feel the fell of dark, not day.
What hours, O what black hoürs we have spent
This night! what sights you, heart, saw; ways you went!
And more must, in yet longer light's delay.
            With witness I speak this. But where I say
Hours I mean years, mean life. And my lament
Is cries countless, cries like dead letters sent
To dearest him that lives alas! away.

            I am gall, I am heartburn. God's most deep decree
Bitter would have me taste: my taste was me;
Bones built in me, flesh filled, blood brimmed the curse.
            Selfyeast of spirit a dull dough sours. I see
The lost are like this, and their scourge to be
As I am mine, their sweating selves; but worse.

- Gerard Manley Hopkins

Chapter 2

A Crisis Leads to a New Sense of Identity
By Graeme Lauber

Graeme Lauber is a word guy—reading them, writing them, speaking them. He manages communications for Journey and is the Calgary-area program coordinator.

> So Jesus said to them, "Truly I tell you, unless you eat the flesh of the Son of Man and drink his blood, you do not have life in yourselves. The one who eats my flesh and drinks my blood has eternal life, and I will raise him up on the last day, because my flesh is true food and my blood is true drink. The one who eats my flesh and drinks my blood remains in me, and I in him. Just as the living Father sent me and I live because of the Father, so the one who feeds on me will live because of me. This is the bread that came down from heaven; it is not like the manna your ancestors ate—and they died. The one who eats this bread will live forever."

-John 6:53-58

I'm a fan of weird passages of Scripture. If you grew up with Sunday School like I did, you tended to hear the same stories over and over again. For example, you heard all about Noah's flood, and I was absolutely clear in my own mind that Noah brought two of every kind of animal onto the ark except for the clean animals—he loaded up seven of those. What I don't remember learning, in Sunday School or anywhere else, was about all the serious family dysfunction that happened after Noah and the kids got off the boat. This was not considered appropriate for Sunday mornings, even if it was in the Bible.

Those of us who know our Bibles know that the Noah story is in the Old Testament, which describes the time before Jesus came. However, once Jesus is on the scene, it feels like the Bible becomes a little more socially acceptable. We know Jesus mostly talks about loving our neighbours and being nice to one another, so we no longer worry about reading anything that might shock the elderly. However, Jesus actually said a lot of very weird and difficult things Himself—and we often find ourselves avoiding passages, just like we've done with Noah.

One of the weird things Jesus says is in John 6. All this talk of eating human flesh and drinking human blood is shocking, so we've worked very hard for the last couple of thousand years to tone it down a bit so that middle class people don't get upset and think Jesus is some sort of freak. This saying of Jesus is hard to understand, and I find myself having to wrestle with what He actually said, rather than what I wish He'd said. According to N.T. Wright, when Jesus says that we should eat His flesh, He uses a word that means something like "munch," suggesting that He wants us to eat Him with gusto, to really enjoy eating Him[1]. This makes me uncomfortable.

Jesus' audience didn't have small, tasteless wafers of bread and teensy cups of grape juice to help make them feel okay with what Jesus was saying. I had Sunday School teachers who were able to make passages like this super-spiritual, which is another way of

---

[1] N. T. Wright, *John for Everyone* (2004).

saying they made it totally irrelevant. Jesus' audience didn't have that option. They were left to wonder why Jesus would use a weird, gross, and somewhat offensive image to describe what it would be like to follow Him.

The image of eating Jesus' flesh and drinking His blood is shocking, especially to a people who were very careful about what they ate, including avoiding blood of any kind. But it's also very intimate. In fact, it is partly this intimacy that makes the image uncomfortable for us. Jesus doesn't just want to be our friend, and He doesn't just want to be our Lord. He doesn't just want to be the one who carries us along the beach when we're too tired to walk ourselves. In fact, He doesn't just want to be our Saviour (although of course He wants to be all of these things). He wants to be our food—He wants to live inside us and to feed us so that all our desires are fulfilled. He wants to gratify us, so that we're so taken with Him that we never really worry about getting a decent meal ever again.

When I say that Jesus wants to give us something deeper and more gratifying than anything else that is available, images of my Sunday School teachers come before my eyes. (The poor women who taught me Sunday School—they were all such great people, trying so hard. I actually don't have a specific person in mind, this is just how we all thought about Christianity for a long time.) They were always talking about how knowing Jesus was more satisfying than going to school dances, but I snuck into a few school dances—I think I'm forgiven for this, but I'm not totally sure—and I think they were pretty satisfying. (It shows how deprived I really was as a kid that I found junior high school dances satisfying as opposed to sweaty and awkward). Christianity was about performance, it was about ethics, it was about being good, well-behaved young men and women.

This view makes it seem like God is a cosmic kill-joy—taking away things like partying and alcohol when I was young, and money and prestige when my tastes "matured." The one area where there was consistent struggle was in my sexuality. There was always a big difference between what I believed God wanted and what I wanted. I decided that this simply meant that I would have to miss out on having my desires met, I would have to learn to live with lack.

Eventually, however, the lack caught up with me. A few years ago, I found myself attending this church that I really loved. Eventually the pastors came to the church's leadership team (of which I was a member) with the idea that we become "affirming"—a church that believes God endorses and blesses gay relationships. They said that they would eventually like to come to the point where they could perform gay weddings.

This threw me into a massive crisis. I had always believed that the Bible taught that homosexual behaviour was sinful, but now my pastors were telling me that we might have been wrong about that. They were telling me that my sexuality *was* my identity, who I was. My Christianity had always been ethical—it was about how I behaved, not who I was, so I had no firmly-established identity of my own. For the first time I began to think seriously about my sexual identity, and I began to build a gay identity for myself. I then began to question all the choices I had made—was my marriage a mistake? Was my family? How should I live if this is who I am? I began to use gay identity to help answer these questions, but that created a new problem. I felt like I was splitting in two—there was the husband and father and then there was this gay man, who was not the marrying sort. This split was very painful, and the only way I knew to manage it was with addiction—pornography, drugs, and alcohol.

And then Jesus intervened.

After a couple of years, I found myself in a Journey Discipleship Course. I was aware very early on that there was nothing I could say about myself that would cause my Journey leaders to turn their backs on me. I was able to be honest about my struggles with identity, and with same-sex attractions, and with addiction. And then we just prayed together, in community.

During prayer at Journey, Jesus asked me to give up my gay identity and, in fact, to sacrifice any right I might have to define myself. This is the hardest thing I have ever done. I needed my gay identity by that point. It was how I understood myself, and I didn't know who I was without it. So, my reaction to Jesus was, "No, you can't have that, I need that. I don't know how to go on without it." But in prayer, I was eventually able to say "yes" and that "yes" felt like having the heart ripped right out of me.

But Jesus came to me in that moment, and He filled up all the empty spaces in my life that my gay identity had been filling. I sensed Him in a new way, and my relationship with Him has never been the same. He took this split person and began putting him back together. My identity issues were not immediately solved, but now it was Jesus and me working on my identity, in community with people who loved me and cared for me.

For others, the details of what God is calling them to may be different, but the outline is the same. Many people have tried to live the Christian life and found it frustrating and sterile. This is often due to the fact that they are trying to live according to Christian ethics without living out of Christian identity. People often want to *look* like Christians, even if they don't *feel* like Christians. They believe Christianity is true, but they may not think it's real. When we try to live like Christians (giving to the poor, controlling our temper, not lusting) but it feels like a slog, we end up in despair. We've learned about Jesus, but we haven't munched on His body.

For many years, I was caught in a trap of thinking Jesus wants to take things away from me—He often seemed dour and opposed to fun. Much like the story of Noah and the ark, I had part of the story clear in my mind—that following Jesus included big personal sacrifice. But just like the Noah story, I had not got the full picture. I missed the parts where Jesus says that He wants to provide something deeper and more satisfying than anything in this world. He wants to have Himself in us; He wants to have Himself in me, and He wants me to be in Him. He wants all of us to be "in Christ." I want to be like one of Jesus' early listeners— someone who is both shocked and intrigued.

Chapter 3

Wanting More—and Finding It
by Dave Erickson

Dave Erickson has never found pizza better than that made in his hometown of Chicago. He and his wife Tracy have two young adult children. Dave is the founder of Pancaran Anugerah (Journey Indonesia).

You've likely at some time been part of this standard youth group exercise: make two lists; one of personal "needs," the other of "wants." The meeting's topic probably is intercessory prayer, and you must sort between the two. It is a fun exercise, especially when you let your imagination run wild with your list of wants... three new cars, a lake house, iPhone 15-Pro, speedboat, new snow skis, and a box filled with a zillion dollars! The conclusion of the Bible study is usually that God delights in answering prayers regarding needs but is quite ambivalent about all those wants!

In Journey we talk a lot about need. Our programs begin focused on ways in which basic psychological needs such as love, affirmation, and attention were not filled in early childhood. Then, for years afterwards, we have tried to fill those gaps in healthy and unhealthy ways. Looking at human life, we first notice essential needs like food, water, sleep, and oxygen. Later we see broader aspirations for respect, freedom, accomplishment and, for some, a mug of hot coffee in the morning. We do have a lot of needs!

Do We Notice?

Our personal needs long hide under the surface of our hearts. This is often the case when we are younger and lack the breadth of life experience and relationships needed for maturity. Nothing is wrong with that. Our awareness emerges and accumulates slowly, eventually reaching a point where we can no longer ignore them. Awareness of my own wounds, loneliness, and need for love did not begin until I was in university and interacting with a wider variety of people. When I began to struggle in friendships and communication, I began to wonder why.

Have you noticed how awareness of need emerges very pointedly in times of crisis? During a pandemic or a week-long electrical outage, for example. After a heated argument with a friend, I need your listening ear. While walking on an icy sidewalk, I need your hand. When grieving the loss of a family member, I need your hug.

My family has lived in Indonesia for many years. One of the challenges of driving there is the many open drainage ditches at the sides of the roads. One day I was picking up my daughter from her painting lesson. As I backed my car down a narrow lane, the car suddenly jerked to a stop, and the front end jumped up half a meter. I knew immediately what had happened. I also knew immediately that I was NOT going to ask for help! I would be quiet, inconspicuous as possible, and use my own amazing musculature to quickly lift that 2000kg car right out of the ditch.

Well, that did not happen. The store owner near the ditch shouted an alarm and, soon, eight young men arrived, eager to help me out of my dilemma. I needed help. It was obvious to all. My feeling of shame (and stupidity) was completely overcome by desperation. I could not help myself.

Never Enough

As a young adult I began to be aware of that deep lack of affection and affirmation. Not only had I been building relationships based primarily on my own unmet needs, but I was riddled with anxiety and paralyzed when faced with big decisions at new stages of life. Could I fulfill what that potential job required? Could I meet the demands of greater responsibility? Could someone like me be a leader, husband, father? Really?

Then I had an encounter with God. Up to that point in my life I had, unfortunately, built a rather thick wall of resentment toward my dad. He had, in fact, offered me some of the good stuff I needed to grow well in life, but I had usually rejected his offerings of love and affirmation. It took me a long time of blaming him before I realized my part in actively refusing the good he had tried to give to me.

One night in prayer, God showed me "the wall" and nudged me to forgive and turn my heart toward my dad. As I hesitantly did that, I could sense that parts of that wall were weakening, and through new gaps in the wall flowed a portion of the love I had so long waited for.

Ah. That was nice! A part of me was satisfied. But my heart again cried out to God. "I'm very thankful, but my soul is still so thirsty, Father. I need so much more!" With great certainty God told me He had more to give. He had what I needed. He was so very proud of me and promised to be with me in each new challenge and responsibility I was given.

Those experiences of divine generosity are milestones—moments of awesome infilling, healing, and hope. Yet, we know that gaps still exist even as we imperfectly process triggers, build intimacy in friendship, and wait in God's presence for more. Our hearts still crave. As the gospel singer calls, "I need Thee, O I need Thee. Every hour I need Thee."

Among the privileges of still being in process and experiencing need is the opportunity to be humble, to be gentle, to let go, and to empathize with others who are also on their own thirsty journey with Jesus. Your unending neediness is a gift to the Body of Christ and one of your valuable personal blessings from God!

My favorite poetic expression of longing is in Psalm 63. The images of thirst and desperation speak to my condition: "Earnestly I seek you; I thirst for you, my whole being longs for you, in a dry and parched land where there is no water." A confession of the obsessed: "I think of you through the watches of the night." Like a newborn baby: "I cling to you; your right hand upholds me."

Not Sovereign

As profound and urgent as our needs may be, they never absolutely define our identity. I am not the "one who was neglected" but, more accurately, "the one who has been adopted and loved." Need is not sovereign in anyone's life.[2] Need can cause pain and lead us into a heap of trouble, but it is not destiny. God's work of love, grace, freedom, rescue, restoration, and hope are definitive. God remains sovereign. Jesus' death on the cross and resurrection to New Life speak of our destiny.

There is always a limit to need, sin, mistakes, and ignorance. Because the love of God has triumphed in Jesus, we do not need to move into a panicked desperation. We do not hide in shame. Love's sure work gives us permission to relax, let go, smile, and even rest from the hard work of transformation.

As I look back at my life I often chuckle with amusement. Despite my many gaps and errors, God has allowed me to be a good enough husband, a good enough father, and an okay friend to a few. God has been sovereign over it all and has been able to override the impact of so much of what is not quite right in my life.

---

[2] Toni Kim. "Pastoral Care Doesn't Require Capes" *Christianity Today* (Spring, 2021) https://www.christianitytoday.com/pastors/2021/spring/pastoral-care-doesnt-require-capes-heroes.html

My life's compass has swung more firmly to the pole of Magnetic Love than to the pole of neediness and brokenness.

This fact is important for those of us involved in ministries of pastoral care. The brokenness of those we meet is not sovereign. God is. His grace is active in their lives every day. So, a bit of healthy detachment and forgetfulness of "problems" is necessary and rejuvenating. We do not need to be forever probing, identifying, and solving those needs. God's work of freedom and transformation have the upper hand.

From the Beginning, a Stirring

So, at what moment does God intervene for people who are in need? Many accuse God of being late, if not completely absent and unconcerned. If, like me, you prefer to think linearly you might imagine this timeline: I am alive. Big smile. I face personal loss. Big frown. I ask God for help. God responds and arrives at my side with the first aid kit. Does God only show up on the scene, like emergency rescue vehicle do, once there has been a fatal explosion? I do not believe that God teases us and waits until life has completely broken down. A less linear understanding is perhaps more accurate: "You are in me, and I am in you,"[3] "I will never leave you,"[4] "In him we live and move and have our being."[5]

I suggest that from the beginning, in surprising ways, Love makes Itself known in hunger pangs and the feeling of incompleteness. That uncomfortable, stinging feeling is itself a grace. God, somehow present in that sting, stirs within our souls. This stir and call of Love brings us to awareness and brings openness to His intervention. There is great value and dignity to our experiences of need.

---

[3] John 14, John 15
[4] Heb. 13:5
[5] Acts 17:28

Can we imagine this being a way God is involved in our lives? God has always been with us, alongside our need. When we request help, His love is actualized—made concrete. God neither immediately relieves us of our needs nor forces help upon us. Unmet needs are uncomfortable. But we can be sure that the gnawing distress of need is not only motivation to seek God's help but also a reminder that God is at this very moment embracing us in these most precious areas of our lives. Both God's acts of discipline and his great "bear hugs" can indeed be uncomfortable moments of transformation.

Chapter 4

No Longer Listening to Lies
by Toni Dolfo-Smith

Toni Dolfo-Smith is a Vancouver-based artist. He is the founder and executive director of Journey Canada and Journey Global.

I have never been a prolific journal processor, but over the last 35 years or so, I have kept what I have jokingly referred to as a "loose journal." On an infrequent basis I record important events in my life, agonizing and spewing in times of crisis, wondering and musing during more reflective times and sometimes just wasting another page with self-piteous drivel! I have never been one to revisit and reread what I have written—my process has been simple—I write and then leave well enough alone.

A few years ago, the spiritual director who was walking alongside me during my sabbatical suggested that the time of rest and reflection presented a good opportunity to reread my old journals, beginning a couple of years prior to my marriage, travelling through the early years of starting Journey, up until about three years before my sabbatical began.

I must confess that I was initially reluctant—okay, I was inwardly repulsed at the idea, already anticipating the shame I would feel when reading what I had written! I certainly did bump into some of that shame as I waded through the embarrassing, brooding teen-like angst (did a 25-year-old really write that?), meandering introspection and cringeworthy "insights." However, beyond the embarrassment, I also encountered an unexpected surprise. Coursing through my writing was the 35-year history of the journey of a shame-based, insecure young man who was once very protective of his image, into a more mature man (I hope), living beyond the shame that had once dominated and dictated his life.

Until that point, speaking about shame was a familiar part of my teaching repertoire. When speaking at various events, I had regularly recounted personal stories of experiencing shame and the ongoing healing of that shame. But rereading those journals made me see that journey through an entirely new lens.

I know that I experienced shame from the very beginning of my life, but it was at five years of age that I recall my first vivid encounter with shame. I had no name for it then, but that first encounter would set the stage for a lifetime battle—emotional, physical and spiritual—with life destroying shame. That shame would become my constant companion, questioning, undermining, and eroding the real me.

The story goes something like this—I was in a store with my mother when the store owner, speaking in another language, gestured excitedly toward me and started saying things that were quite obviously about me. While I comprehended some of what was being said, I did not have the vocabulary to understand certain words. I remember my five-year-old self feeling quite confused and anxious as we left the store and I could also tell that my mother herself was flustered and embarrassed. I asked her what the words that the store owner had used meant. I remember her kind and sad face as she looked at me, and reassured me that she loved me completely, but that the store owner had said that I was an unattractive little boy!

I have lived that moment too many times to mention—the shock, the horror, and the shame that blanketed me as we walked home. Years later I would finally hear the truth, which as you have probably guessed was quite the opposite of what my mom had conveyed to me. The store owner had, in fact, enthusiastically complimented my mother on her handsome young son. My mom's own shame, and her fear that compliments like that would develop pride, arrogance and superiority in me prompted her to say what she did, not realizing that she had directed me down a road of pain and suffering that would affect so much of my life. I now had a travelling companion called Shame who would work tirelessly at reshaping my self-identity.

Shame, as I have often stated, is not the feeling that I've done something bad or embarrassing. It's the feeling that I AM bad, that there is something intrinsically wrong with me. Having been raised in a racially-mixed family in South Africa, by the age of five I was already acutely aware that my skin colour was different than the rest of my cousins, and that I was prohibited from attending the same schools, parks, restaurants, and beaches as they were. My mother's pronouncement simply confirmed what I already knew… I was defective!

From that moment, Shame would mock and then eventually destroy my natural childlike exuberance and inquisitiveness. Shame would force me to inhibit and restrain my emotions to ensure that I presented as someone who would be acceptable to others. Shame would constantly whisper to remind me that I was being silly, stupid, or making a fool of myself. While most other emotions have a natural physical release and outlet that allows them to be released, Shame does not. It never leaves—it simply remains with us as our constant unwelcome companion.

By the time I emerged into young adulthood, Shame had succeeded in fully convincing me that who I was, was not enough. If I was to succeed, I needed to present an image of who I wanted others to see me as. My internalized shame made me dislike my real self, leaving me mired in anger, rage, anxiety, and despair. The only "solution" was a whole new image—a False Self. But this image feared being discovered and rejected as an imposter, which further alienated me from real people and life-giving friendships. I was left grasping for something to make me feel better, and this desperate and insatiable need eventually led to the development of a secret life of addiction and false comfort. Without realizing it, I was stuck in a cyclical bog of heaving toxic shame.

Though I had had a very real encounter with God in my late teens, Shame had sufficiently convinced me that the only respectable way to approach God was through my False Self. The irony of course is that my real self desperately yearned for renewal and revival but was never good enough to be brought to God. The real me remained unchanged and untouched.

Shame cannot simply be eradicated by a prayer or a prophecy, nor will it ever leave because it is told to. I saw that in stark relief as I read my journals—Shame can only be usurped by a more compelling voice.

That Voice first whispered to me at a point in life when I had made an uneasy truce with Shame. That Voice kept telling me that there was more for me, that my real self could actually be reclaimed. With a courage I never knew I had, and risking the wrath of Shame, I chose to voluntarily listen and obey that Voice. For a long time a struggle ensued between that Voice and Shame's efforts to reclaim me. Shame shrieked and yelled that I was making a mistake, that what I was experiencing was not real. But that Voice calmy reassured me that He was with me and that He would never leave me. He was no longer just that Voice, but the person of Jesus who walked with me, my new travelling companion.

As I read through my journals during my time of rest, I would often cry when I recalled certain incidents and occurrences, and the ways in which Jesus had spoken to me. As I read on, I could see that Shame never relented in its efforts to reclaim me. Often, it seemed that when I was navigating the most precarious and vulnerable parts of my journey, Shame would lunge out and attempt to destabilize any sure footing. I saw, too, that I was most vulnerable when I chose not to listen to Jesus and instead chose my own introspective ruminations to become the voice that guided me. Remarkably, I could clearly see the point where Shame could no longer fully convince me that I was not who He says I am!

Over a period of two months, I continued reading those journals. I was honestly amazed by the clear progression I could see in my writings—not in my writing style, but in the knowledge that the only way to leave Shame behind was to let Jesus lead me and tell me who I truly was. I read incident after incident where I struggled with doubt and shame, being rescued again and again by Jesus—a wealth of new illustrations for my talks on shame.

In many ways I could see the birth, growth, and development of the ministry of Journey as a parallel path to my own personal journey away from Shame. There have been so many issues Jesus has continued to heal in me, but probably none as entangled with my personhood as my relationship with Shame. My journals show that as I walked with Jesus, the distance between Shame and I grew increasingly wide. Did the voice of Shame stop speaking to me? No, it has not. What I hear now, though, are no longer the edicts and commands I once felt compelled to follow. Shame's attempts at my derailment have lost steam.

I have re-read my journals a couple of times since my sabbatical, and over and over I have seen the faithful, relentless pursuit of Jesus. Never shouting, never combative, but always reassuring, always invitational. The compelling, clear, calm voice of Jesus has prevailed, and continues to assure me of who I am in Him.

Chapter 5

Escaping the Swamp
by Andrew Lakin

Andrew Lakin is a communicator who knows more about trees and the Muppets than is really necessary. He is a former Journey coordinator and staff member. He and his family live in Stratford, Ontario.

This chapter is called "Sin." Not very catchy, is it? We are all tempted to sin, just as you are tempted to skip this chapter because no one likes reading about sin. It's ok. I'm not offended. Well maybe a little, but I'll make sure I receive some prayer for that later.

I grew up thinking of sin as "doing bad stuff." But sin can even be something good that we have corrupted by making it an ultimate thing, like food. There can be many things that we reach for to bring us comfort that are outside of God's design for us. Sin can become our source, our protector; sin can even come to feel like a friend.

I was introduced to pornography at an early age. I had so many cycles of victory and failure. I remember making so many resolutions. Times of repentance at the youth retreat, and I would come home and burn it all (this was back when pornography was on paper). And I declared, "Never again! You and me God, we've got this!" But then the cycle would come back around, and there I would go, escaping into fantasy and porn. I began to think that this was just me, my design, and I could never escape it.

27

My mother struggled with depression for 13 years. I remember her saying that this was her normal now. And I hated that because I remembered a time when she was not depressed, and was so much more full-of-life.

I remember thinking, "She's like me."

Let me be clear. I am not saying depression is sin. It was just, for me, I saw her depression and my addiction as having a similar acceptance of a new normal that God wanted to set us free from.

I remember her saying that she didn't see hope of change, that she accepted this as her world. I felt the same. I felt that we were both sinking in our own swamps; my mother in her swamp of sadness, and me in my swamp of pornography addiction, wondering if freedom actually exists.

I sat down and wrote this poem:

The Swamp

elbow deep

> *to the biceps tomorrow*
mosquitoes   stench   compost   sludge   mold

> *How did I get here?*
> *I don't know*
> *It's just kind of... where I live*
> *Was I put here?*
>> *or did I... did I choose it?*

it's a slow subtle sinking
it's a slow subtle stinking

I hardly notice the bacteria decaying my flesh
> *flesh decaying my soul*

>> *been told there's a hand*
>>> *I may have even seen it before*
but it's been too long
and I'm too deep

smelling as bad as I do no one would want to be near me
> *- much less pull me out*

I have called for help before
> *when the sinking was fast*

no one came

> *I've been here so long*
>> *it's become the only world I understand*

and you know what?

>> *It's not so bad*

the slime's not as gross as it seems really
and I got used to the stench ages ago

I've spent most of my life here
> *It's*
> *become*
> *my life*

I think I once lived a walking running life
> > *but it was so long ago*
> > *I wonder if I dreamed it*
> > *Yeah*

What
You think I like being stuck here?
> *slowly sinking*
> *slowly rotting*

of course not

> > *But*
> *deep down inside*
> > *I wonder if I love it*

> > *just because I know it*

and I hate myself for knowing it

> *but*
> > *it's all that I know.*

Maybe you resonate with some of that. Maybe you've had a time in your life when something repugnant to you brought you comfort and, maybe, over time, started to feel like home.

Fast forward five years. My mother's depression finally broke. How? Someone prayed for her. Why did it work that time, and not the other thousands of times someone prayed for her? I have no idea, and I guess I'll have to ask God when I get to heaven.

At the same time, I had hit rock bottom in my struggle with pornography. All my attempts to "fix it" myself had failed. I was desperate, but desperation can be a very good thing as a catalyst for change. At this time, a guy had stood up in church and been— gasp— honest. He spoke about how he had been abused. I could not get over how vulnerable he was, at CHURCH. I knew I had to be a part of the discipleship ministry he was sharing about, and I signed up for the Journey program at my church.

I caught a strange scent in the fall air. It was Hope.

During the program, I began to allow God into some of those dark, murky, embarrassing places, and He began to slowly bring some healing. During this time, my mother, who had never heard my Swamp poem, nor knew about the program I was taking, called and left a message on my answering machine. This is what she said:

> I waited patiently for the LORD;
> he turned to me and heard my cry.
> He lifted me out of the slimy pit,
> out of the mud and mire;
> he set my feet on a rock
> and gave me a firm place to stand.
> He put a new song in my mouth,
> a hymn of praise to our God.

-Psalm 40:1-3a (NIV)

I wept then. I weep now. That was 30 years ago. Today, it is the ongoing work of surrender; continuing to look to God for my hope, my comfort, my security, my identity (it's a long list).

Sometimes I am tempted to return to that swamp. Doesn't that sound gross? How could that be? I have tasted freedom and the walking running life. But it does call to me like an old toxic friend. I have to remind myself, Jesus has a backhoe and He filled in that swamp. Then He planted a garden and flowers, and built a playground, where He continues to invite me to come and play. I imagine there may still be some swampiness farther out there if I want to go look for it, but I would have to walk through the playground to get to it.

This is my discipleship: to surrender, and daily choose to come and play.

Chapter 6

Chains
Confronting Some Necessary Pain
by Becca Brunner

Becca Brunner is a seminary student and pastor who has worked with Journey in a variety of roles. She lives in Burnaby, British Columbia.

I remember the first several years of my spiritual walk being full of contradictions and conflicting emotions. Getting to know Jesus was exciting and beautiful but it was difficult following Him, too. I felt especially convicted over my sexual behaviour and felt called by Jesus to give it up, to live a chaste life. I was genuinely committed to doing this, to trying at least, but I felt burdened by exhaustion and the emotional toll it was taking on me. This was confusing because I had read the Gospels and understood Jesus' ministry as one of freedom. I saw how Jesus met people in their sickness, oppression, isolation, and sinfulness and how He set them free, leading them into greater life. I had encountered this same Jesus for myself in a real and profound way and yet I was feeling less free than I had before. What was going on?

If you are like me and you have made it this far in your spiritual walk, you are likely aware of the necessity to confront your sin. You know that you have tried to meet your needs on your own and have turned away from the Father. It is hard, but you are committed to the ongoing process of repentance and re-orienting yourself towards God. But this is where things got tricky for me. It seemed like the more I tried to do this, the more I tried to change my behaviour, the more entrenched it became. I was just as bound up in my sexual behaviour as ever, only now I was also completely worn out from fighting it. It took me a long time to realize what the process of repentance would actually mean for me, because I did not understand the extent to which I was dependent upon my sexual behaviour for survival.

Before my dad started working with eating disorder patients as a therapist, he used to work shifts on the addiction ward at the hospital. He once told me about a homeless man who was admitted for medical observation while he was detoxing from alcohol. He was dirty and unkempt after having slept outside for years, but he was too sick from withdrawals to bathe himself. As the nurses undressed him, they found that some of his clothes were stiff and difficult to remove. When they got to his socks, they discovered they could not remove them at all. His socks had completely fused with his feet so that taking them off would mean ripping away the man's skin.

This is what the process of repentance is actually like. Some things we hand over to Jesus fairly easily, other things with more difficulty, and still others leave us feeling naked and exposed. But then there are those coping mechanisms which we are deeply attached to, which have become a part of us, so that becoming free of them will take time and a great deal of pain—like tearing our skin away.

Our coping mechanisms are, in many ways, what have gotten us through life up until this point. They have sustained us in our emptiness and pain, shielding us from the realization that our problems are far more serious than whatever our presenting behaviour may be. The thing we are attached to in itself might not even be bad. For example, money, family, career, and food are all good things, but our reliance on anything other than God will keep us from following Jesus freely. In the end, we are no better off for using our work to cope than the person who drinks every day in order to get by.

The way forward is not to try and manage our behaviour like I tried to do. That will only leave us feeling exhausted. We have to be honest about the reality of our situation and our inability to do anything about it. We are responsible to own up to our attachments, but we need to turn to God if we are going to live without them. We cannot schedule our coping mechanisms out of our lives, we cannot rely on our own strength and self-sufficiency, and we cannot displace our ways of coping with more socially acceptable ones. The only way forward is to acknowledge the full extent of our coping behaviours and then let them go.

Letting go means stepping into the unknown, stripped of our devices, where we learn the depths of our weakness and need for God. Here we reclaim our profound emptiness and longing, even that which is broken, and turn to God in surrender. There is no exact formula for doing this and we cannot know what the road ahead will entail or the desolation we may experience. If we were to know how God intended to meet us in the absence of our coping mechanisms then we would be inclined to continue the trek alone. Jesus knows that what we are yearning for is Himself and so He will not allow us to find freedom without Him.

Jesus has made freedom possible but He will not force it upon us. He honours our free will by giving us the responsibility to choose for ourselves whether or not we will continue along in our spiritual journey. Just like the story of the rich young ruler in Matthew 19 who would not give up his wealth, Jesus will let us walk away if we decide the cost of following Him is too great. As we wrestle and grapple with the choice at hand, we must remember that whatever loss we might experience is so that we are available to receive all the fullness of life and joy that Jesus offers.

Chapter 7

A Physician Learns Wound Care
by Doris Barwich

Doris Barwich, MD is a strategic leader who served on Journey Canada's Board for many years as well as being involved with small group leadership and teaching. She is committed to enabling others to walk in freedom and wholeness.

For many years, I was defined by wounds inflicted by emotional, physical, and early sexual abuse. Raised in a conservative Christian family as the eldest of five children, my role was to care for the needs of others. Looking good and doing and saying the right things was very important, so I learned early on to bury my pain and the truth about what had happened to me throughout my childhood and teen years. This resulted in a very capable, bright, pretty girl on the outside, but on the inside, I was vulnerable to those who offered me safety, love, and belonging. As an adult I was not aware of the ways in which my childhood experiences dictated my choices. After two abusive marriages, desperate for answers, I entered the Journey Canada 26-week discipleship program to find a different way forward.

I will never forget my first night there. At the beginning of the evening, about 20 leaders shared their personal testimonies of sexual and relational brokenness and how God had encountered them and dramatically transformed their lives. I remember thinking that I did not know or understand the radical love and grace that would allow for that level of authenticity. Theirs were stories of profound hope. If God could do that for them, then perhaps there was hope for me. That night I committed to a journey of obedience and courage—to let God more fully into my life. I was determined to come out of hiding and seek truth and healing. I could no longer live in denial.

As I reflect on the process now, I can see that the journey actually began several years earlier. One Sunday morning in church, I had heard the Lord say to me, "You have been saying 'no' to me and you need to start saying 'yes'." I had been doing the best I knew how—striving to be a good Christian but feeling hopeless, trapped in patterns of abandonment, betrayal, and exploitation. I had not realized that despite all my prayer, Bible study, and church activity I had somehow been saying "No" to God. He was telling me I had choices and asking for my "Yes." As I explored this statement, I understood that saying "Yes" to Him would be as simple as making time to listen for His voice of truth and allow Him to love and heal me. And that night, for the first time, I felt like a door of hope had opened. I was not alone and felt surrounded by others who shared aspects of my story and would become a safe, supportive environment for me to heal.

Over the next 26+ weeks of worship, Biblical teaching, and small group times, I began to get in touch with deep places of wounding. Places where emotional needs had not been met, walled-off places, and places where the sins of others had deeply wounded me and created trauma triggers. Through the prayer ministry of my small group leader and others, I was supported to meet Jesus in the painful memories of my past. Over and over, as I met Jesus, He was just waiting for my "Yes," to welcome Him into my pain. I came to understand that He is God with me and has always been with me. He sees me just as I am. He sees my pain and wounding and offers me hope and healing. Jesus also suffered abandonment and betrayal and He not only understood my pain, He also made provision for it at the cross. In every place of wounding, He offers healing, freedom, and hope.[6] Instead of seeing myself as broken, I came to understand that my wounds represented areas of my life where God's truth and love have not yet penetrated and asserted their dominion. I could choose to come to Him and accept what He was offering, to be part of His family and to receive what I had always longed for—acceptance, love, and connection.

Much of my journey into spiritual freedom also involved allowing the Holy Spirit to transform my mind. I had embraced deeply embedded lies that there was something inherently wrong with me, that I was disqualified by the abuse I had suffered and that there was no hope for me. Lies that my brokenness was permanent or defining and that I was outside the circle of grace and could never walk in the abundant life I read about in the Bible. I needed to deal with lies about my identity which kept me in bondage and led to painful patterns of thought that kept me locked into cycles of abuse.

Over and over, He invited me to exchange lies for truth. Though my feelings told me I was a powerless victim and an abandoned orphan, it was not the truth. The truth about me was not my wounding—the truth was that God knew me before I was born. His plan for me is one of intimate relationship and blessing and that, in partnership with the Holy Spirit, I am an overcomer. I can embrace my new identity as a deeply loved person who is part of a new family. I also have an advocate and companion who walks with me, step by step, into the abundant life I longed for.

Another important aspect of my healing journey involved understanding the power of forgiveness. Choosing to forgive those who had sinned against me, knowingly or unknowingly, though painful, freed me from bondage. Forgiving myself opened the door to freedom--the freedom to say "no" to powerlessness and a life of bondage and "yes" to a life of freedom and grace. I no longer needed to allow others to define me, use me or exploit me. I could

---

[6] Hosea 2

be seen for who I am without fear. His forgiveness was total and complete, and transformation was possible when I allowed His truth to set me free.

I am reminded of the wound care analogy. For a cut to heal, it requires cleansing and the removal of foreign bodies and dead tissues (lies and unforgiveness). Often stitches (intention and forgiveness) are needed to bring together separated tissues, as well as creating and sustaining an environment for the body to heal (new thoughts and connection to God and to His body). Covering and protecting the repaired wound allows for complete healing and a return to normal function. And, occasionally, deep wounds are left open to heal from the bottom up.

I also needed to learn to trust the Lord when healing did not happen quickly or look like I thought it should. For a long season I needed to make room for painful memories to surface and to process and grieve them at the cross—to identify the lie, embrace the truth, and receive what God had for me in exchange. Fear, shame, self-hatred, condemnation, and self-sufficiency all needed to be replaced by the love and the acceptance that Christ was offering. Emmanuel, God with us, continues to offer me His loving embrace in every place of wounding. He also wants me to walk with others in His body, allowing them to bring authentic connection, acceptance, encouragement, and ongoing provision. I could also offer the comfort and love I have found and make that available to others.

My journey with the Lord is no longer striving for some future perfection but is about appropriating what has already been accomplished at the cross and allowing it to be the truth I live by. I know that the Father, Son, and Holy Spirit are all deeply committed to my wholeness and will not rest until my transformation is complete. Healing of wounds and new life in Christ are possible.

Chapter 8

The Past
Lessons from a Slave
by Rosemary Flaaten

Rosemary Flaaten is a Calgary-based leader, speaker and author. She currently serves as a member of Journey's board of directors.

> "Where have you come from and where are you going?"
>
> -Genesis 16:8

Those were the questions the angel of the Lord asked Hagar as she sat by a spring in the desert. Hagar's response provides a glimpse into her tumultuous situation. She was an Egyptian handmaiden to Sarai and a concubine to Sarai's husband Abram. This polygamous situation was Sarai's plan for providing an heir for Abram. It is doubtful that Hagar had any voice to resist or speak up against the idea. Her new status as "second wife" and now "first pregnant wife" provoked envy and abuse from Sarai, prompting Hagar to flee the very household where she should have experienced protection and care.

So where had she come from? Let's just say, it was complicated!

"Where have you come from?" I struggle to unwind my story so ladened with memories—some joyful and others incredibly sad; some anxiety-inducing and others that bring an involuntary smile to my face.

As a young child, my home seemed rather idyllic. I was the youngest of four children, with parents who, to my recollection, loved each other. We all worked hard on the small family farm in southern Saskatchewan. Faith, family, and music were woven into almost every daily endeavor. If the telling of the story could stop there, I truly could say "and they lived happily ever after."

But life continued. Life changed. Anger and fighting erupted between my dad and brother. My mom's cognitive capabilities started to deteriorate, eventually receiving a presumed diagnosis of early onset Alzheimer's Disease. My two oldest siblings, who made me feel loved and safe, moved on to lives of their own. I found myself in a highly volatile family, struggling to create some semblance of peace, afraid of anyone catching a glimpse that there were problems. As a young teen, I came to believe that if I conveyed any personal needs, they would be the proverbial straw that would cause our family to completely implode. I could hardly wait to graduate from high school and move somewhere, anywhere, in order to get away from the abuse, dysfunction, and heartache that characterized my "where did you come from?"

Fast forward and you find me in the desert; forty years of wandering as I tried to make sense of the life that I could only access through the rear-view mirror. I knew the fumes of the toxic relationships lingered. I knew I bore the emotional scars of the abuse. I could feel my deep unmet needs and my valiant but highly dysfunctional attempts to satisfy my needs. I had long-suffered through a warped body image, self hatred, and shame. My life seemed to be a tangled mess and much of it was connected back to my family of origin.

The temptation is to blame. Pointing the proverbial finger seems as much reactive as deliberate. I, like Hagar, felt completely alone, struggling under the weight of my past. I had carried it so long that I did not know how to differentiate myself from the fear and shame of that little girl, or the independent self-reliant woman that I adeptly projected. I knew how I saw myself, but I had no idea who

God said I was. I could not see a future that was any different from my past. I thought I was doomed to remain bound to my history.

All of us have a starting point—family of origin—that played a huge part in shaping and misshaping who we are today. The things that happened to us, the people close to us, and the choices we made have all shaped our present condition. This isn't unique to humans; it is true of rocks as well.

My husband and I enjoy hiking in the Rocky Mountains. With longer legs and stronger fitness, he can bound up the side of a mountain much more quickly than I can. However, I have discovered a way to ensure I can get a rest part way up the mountain. All I have to do is draw his attention to a rock formation and then ask him to tell me about it. My geologically-trained husband can go on for great lengths about the various forces of nature responsible for laying down organic material that created that particular rock formation. Every rock has a history that can be described when the quarry is exposed, which then also dictates how that rock will be used. Even rocks have a "Where have you come from and where are you going?" story. Isaiah acknowledges this and presents an opportunity to join the past and the future.

> Listen to me, you who pursue righteousness,
> you who seek the LORD:
> Look to the rock from which you were cut,
> and to the quarry from which you were dug.
> Look to Abraham your father,
> and to Sarah who gave birth to you.

> -Isaiah 51:1-2

As we seek to understand the places we come from, the harmful and misshaping effect they have on us, we can offer all of that to Jesus to redeem, restore, and use. By pairing a look into the past with a future of pursuing righteousness and relationship, Isaiah gives us a sketch for how to answer those two seemingly-formidable questions.

Like Hagar, we all stand with one foot firmly planted in the past and the other poised above the future. One question prompts us to look in the rear-view mirror while the other draws our eyes upward from our present reality to look towards the horizon. One is deeply known because it has been lived. The other is completely undetermined. One must be answered by us. Only God can provide a response to the second.

Like Hagar, choices must be made. The question of origin is paired with the question of the future. Hagar was fully aware of where she had come from, but she was uncertain of her future. But as God revealed His plan for her future, she had to decide if she was going to follow His directive. My choice was similar. Would I allow God to provide the answer to the question "Where are you going?" Would I allow Him to provide the next steps as well as the healing that would propel me to take those steps?

In all honesty, sometimes His presence is enough to quickly set my racing, fearful heart at ease and other times my spirit decelerates as I reflect on Jesus. He, better than I or Hagar, knew where He had come from and where He was going. "Jesus knew that the Father had given everything into his hands, that he had come from God, and that he was going back to God."[7] It was this knowledge that allowed Him to trust His Father implicitly so that He could say "Not my will, but yours, be done."[8] It was not a separation, but a merging of the past and the future.

When the past looms large in my mind and the present seems fogged in, Jesus whispers in my ear, "I know where you are going.

---

[7] John13:3
[8] Luke 22:42

I'm already there and I'm preparing you for what you will need in the future. Will you trust me?"

I have learned much in the environment that Journey Canada provides. Sitting and listening for Jesus' perspective has revealed to me that it does not matter the type of rock from which I have been hewn. People and circumstances beyond my control have influenced who I am today. I cannot change any of it. But what I can control is how I choose to respond to it and to what degree I allow God to redeem it and use it. The courage to acknowledge the past, forgive those who have had a misshaping impact on me and then trusting God's good work in me through Jesus, has shifted the trajectory of my life.

It does not matter whether your quarry was rough or brilliant. God takes the things of our past and redeems them for His glory and for the use of His kingdom. When God takes our wounds from the past, heals them and then brings good out of them, we can say along with Paul that, "My imprisonment has had the opposite of its intended effect."[9]

"Where have you come from and where are you going?"

---

[9] Phil. 1:12 MSG

Section 2—Travelling

At the beginning of our journey, when we've taken stock and decided that our coping mechanisms, ignoring pain, and trying to manage things ourselves will no longer work, we are ready to leave "home" and truly travel the spiritual path. Section one was about leaving that home—leaving behind the ways we have been living—and trying to do something new. This next section is about the next steps—now that we've decided to travel, what are we going to do? Where are we going to go?

As followers of Jesus, our attention should now naturally shift from ourselves and our problems to our Saviour. This is not to say that we are unimportant, or that we don't play a role in the relationship, but that we begin to open ourselves up to the ways that He makes himself available to us. We may have felt very alone when we were at home, and we begin to wonder if Jesus is really willing to accompany us. We may have felt unloved, or unworthy, and we want to know if Jesus cares about those things.

At this stage, we may also be asking ourselves, "How?" How do I travel this road? How do I know that I am loved? What are the things I need to know? What do I need to do? What should I understand? In short, how do I advance in the spiritual life?

The chapters in this section provide some guidance when it comes to these questions. They are not small questions, and they have preoccupied the people of God for many millennia, but each writer has taken the opportunity, in their own small way, to speak about one lesson they have learned. A common theme strikes me: We want to know what we must do, and the answer is that we should stop *doing* anything. Instead, we stop and turn our attention to Jesus. We take the opportunity to consider how God parents us, or to accept the friendship of God and His people, or to contemplate the pinnacle of human history, where the love of God met human need in the cross.

-GL

"Supero" by Claude Provost Acrylic on Canvas

In Quest

Have I not voyaged, friend beloved, with thee
On the great waters of the unsounded sea,
Momently listening with suspended oar
For the low rote of waves upon a shore
Changeless as heaven, where never fog-cloud drifts
Over its windless wood, nor mirage lifts
The steadfast hills; where never birds of doubt
Sing to mislead, and every dream dies out,
And the dark riddles which perplex us here
In the sharp solvent of its light are clear?
Thou knowest how vain our quest; how, soon or late,
The baffling tides and circles of debate
Swept back our bark unto its starting-place,
Where, looking forth upon the blank, gray space,
And round about us seeing, with sad eyes,
The same old difficult hills and cloud-cold skies,
We said: 'This outward search availeth not
To find Him. He is farther than we thought,
Or, haply, nearer. To this very spot
Whereon we wait, this commonplace of home,
As to the well of Jacob, He may come
And tell us all things.' As I listened there,
Through the expectant silences of prayer,
Somewhat I seemed to hear, which hath to me
Been hope, strength, comfort, and I give it thee.

'The riddle of the world is understood
Only by him who feels that God is good,
As only he can feel who makes his love
The ladder of his faith, and climbs above
On th' rounds of his best instincts; draws no line
Between mere human goodness and divine,
But, judging God by what in him is best,

With a child's trust leans on a Father's breast,
And hears unmoved the old creeds babble still
Of kingly power and dread caprice of will,
Chary of blessing, prodigal of curse,
The pitiless doomsman of the universe.
Can Hatred ask for love? Can Selfishness
Invite to self-denial? Is He less
Than man in kindly dealing? Can He break
His own great law of fatherhood, forsake
And curse His children? Not for earth and heaven
Can separate tables of the law be given.
No rule can bind which He himself denies;
The truths of time are not eternal lies.'

So heard I; and the chaos round me spread
To light and order grew; and, 'Lord,' I said,
'Our sins are our tormentors, worst of all
Felt in distrustful shame that dares not call
Upon Thee as our Father. We have set
A strange god up, but Thou remainest yet.
All that I feel of pity Thou hast known
Before I was; my best is all Thy own.
From Thy great heart of goodness mine but drew
Wishes and prayers; but Thou, O Lord, wilt do,
In Thy own time, by ways I cannot see,
All that I feel when I am nearest Thee!'

- John Greenleaf Whittier

Chapter 9

The Womb of Relationship with God
by Craig Lockwood

Craig Lockwood is a retired Vineyard Pastor who continues to serve others through inner healing, pastoral counseling, spiritual direction and supervision. He has written material on addiction and spirituality for Journey.

My spiritual life has been a mix. At times I experience God and His nearness but sometimes I have seasons of walking through my days on autopilot—disconnected from God's felt presence. What distracts me? I find myself mesmerized and hardened by my five sense indulgences, my mindless business, and the beckoning to involvement with culture at large. Adrift in this way I am less prayerful and see dimly. I read scripture only to check it off the list. When, through grace, I remember to take time to notice my feelings, I experience the nagging sense that something is missing. Through all my surviving, achieving, and maintaining of everyday life, God seems veiled behind a gauze-like stupor of dulled spirituality. My mind remains active, but I am like a stone skipping over the deep waters where God dwells in my inner temple. I experience a lonely separation from a crucial knowledge of self—the me that dwells in God. Deep calls to deep. I need to heed the deep calling me to return to connection with myself in God.

Habituated, non-circumspect, involvement with our five senses, our unchallenged ways of thinking, our habits of living, and reactions to those around us can be a type of darkness. It can be like sleep-walking in our waking life. "Awake, O sleeper," the scripture exhorts, "and arise from the dead."[10]

What can we do to stay alert and connected to our deep self and the God who loves us? The monk Theophan shared an antidote,

> You must descend from your head to your heart. At present your thoughts of God are in your head. And God Himself is, as it were, outside you, and so your prayer and other spiritual exercises remain exterior. Whilst you are still in your head, thoughts will not easily be subdued but will always be whirling about, like snow in winter or clouds of mosquitoes in the summer. [11]

Indispensable to this descent from head into heart—into deep water—is silence, a retreat from our normal activity. In slowing down, we make space for God to break into the noise in our head. The psalmist cries, "Be still and know I am God."[12] Or my paraphrase, "Stop and notice me!" This needed silencing (slowing) of our external distractions can take various forms: a slow walk in nature, a quiet solitary glass of wine on one's patio, a timer-scheduled review of God-activity in one's day thus far at work, a three-day retreat at a mountain cabin, or time in a special chair that symbolizes a place of meeting with Jesus. Every option is nestled-in consent to God's movement within. Silence means intentional time away from our routine. Sanctuary. We need to enter our "closet" in whatever form it takes. There we reflect on what we have noticed about subtle whispers of the lover of our soul. As one old abbot said to a young novitiate,

---

[10] Eph. 5:14 ESV

[11] Martin Laird, *Into the Silent Land* (2001).

[12] Ps. 46:10 KJV

"Go sit in your cell. Your cell will teach you everything."[13]

Yet, mere stillness is not necessarily the "silence" that we are looking for. We can stop all sensual input and still be carried away by the noise in our brain. Helpful stopping must also include the focus of our will to notice and watch for the activity of God in our life and an intent on listening to what the Holy Spirit wants to show us about God's invitations to us. To watch is to wait.

> But to watch implies more than just waiting. It is not the bored malaise of standing in line at the DMV. It implies attention, yearning, and hope. It's the lover, flowers in hand, searching for that one face in a crowded airport, the expectant mother on alert for the first signs of labor, or the friend pacing outside the operating room.[14]

What is watched for is different for each person depending on how each "hears" God. It might be an inner knowing, a wonder of nature that draws the heart, a spoken phrase that seems to have extra life, a sudden image with noticeable internal power, or a circumstance with an invitation to grow. Once we notice God's subtle movement, we intensify our listening. We remind ourselves that to see more is the gift of God's grace. Increased illumination of the Holy Spirit may take time and unfold slowly, even over days, as we set what we have noticed before our conscious meditation and allow the experience to be amplified. This process connects us to our deepest self in God.

---

[13] Benedicta Ward, *The Desert Christian: Sayings of the Desert Fathers: The Alphabetical Collection* (1980).

[14] Tish Harrison Warren, *Prayer in the Night* (2021).

Becoming habituated to this lifestyle is one aspect of abiding in the vine. It is a place of true rest, a source of gratitude, heightened mystery, a joyous strength, and shalom (peace and harmony).

One such illumination for me started with what might seem like an ordinary walk on the beach with a friend. It was dusk and the sunset was fading. We stayed on the beach as the sky darkened, and the stars intensified. In itself it was a beautiful experience of nature. And yet there was more that God wanted to show me—an experience He wanted to gift to me. The next day the memory seemed to be pressing into my consciousness.

There was an urgency to pay attention to details, images, mood—to receive it more deeply. I began to open to this holy nudging. On the third day, writing about it brought more understanding. A transcendent dimension rose out of my deep heart where the Trinity dwells, and I wrote:

The only light is in front of us.
A captivating, burnt orange oval
indistinctly split where waves meet sky.
Without my awareness it ceases to be a horizon.
Without my permission, an unblinking oracle
now illuminates and searches my soul.

It is a great hall leading to eternity,
whose voice is the multitude of waves
that chant syllables of rising treble
that ebb and flow atop a muted base roar.
I wonder why. Is some great swell coming?
I am transfixed by this unwavering speech
that penetrates my inmost self.

Yet my mind would make wonder small
through grasping for human answers.
Then, I give up analysis and surrender
to being in the moment.
My heart is opening.

Time has stopped.
I am suspended in an alternate dimension
It is the womb of God—always available,
yet always illusive.

I am at once:
Aware that I am lost, and yet feel at home;
Fearing God, and yet wanting more;
Doubting my perception, and yet filled with desire;
Vulnerable and skittish, and yet contained by a great strength;
Humbled by my smallness, but still at peace;
Pierced with awe, and yet present to love.

This union immobilizes and stills me.
And though brightening stars encroach with their dark setting,

cloaking this illumination,
it does not fade in me.
It grows more as the days pass.
At first I cannot comprehend why.

I try to understand, to analyze.
Then I realize this must be contemplation,
which is beyond words.
So I yield to mystery
and let this impartation inform my soul.

Now, this ordinary walk on the beach has been permanently transformed in my memory into a deeply meaningful encounter with God.

One of the definitions of contemplation is to see beyond or to see through. Suddenly what was a distraction might as well be a vehicle of God for connection and illumination. We only need to notice that our God is infused into everything. Illuminated silence is solidifying one's connection to the unseen real. Solitude is not aloneness; it is for connection to the love of the Trinity in real experiential interaction. Life events are seeds. Silence provides the growing season. Reflection and noticing plow the silence. Waiting and watching is incubation. To watch and wait takes time. This way of prayerful practice has been described as "Stop, Look and Listen." It is not automatic. It is, of necessity, a spiritual intention.

The most common resistance to entering silence is that it might be uncomfortable. We protest. What if I feel out of control? What if some painful, undesirable aspect of myself floats to the surface? What if God says something I don't want to hear? All of these scenarios are possible, and yet all are progress towards a deep connection with self and God.

So, what is the process stated concisely? Enter "silence" to make space for God. Notice where and how God seemed to be drawing you towards Himself. Amplify the details through cooperation with the Spirit's gift. Listen for further illumination of where God entered your ordinary life. Receive the gift of contemplation—that of seeing beyond or seeing through. These are the dynamics of silence that lead to the experience of carrying God in the midst of five sense distraction. These are the dynamics that lead to resting in the unseen real.

The promise from Jeremiah 29:13 is true: "You will seek me and find me when you search for me with all your heart."

Chapter 10

The Cross

The Ultimate Paradox

by Eric Stephanson

*E*ric Stephanson is a recovering pastor. He was delighted to grow with Journey for 20 years in many roles.

I grew up not really paying attention to the shape of the wooden cross at the front of the church I attended with my family. So I remember how startled I was to go with a friend one afternoon to a church where a crucifix hung in their empty sanctuary. I was surprised to see the body hung permanently at the front for everyone to see each week. The image stayed with me, in a way that was unpleasant for my ten year old self; today I would say it was too visceral, triggering feelings beyond my capacity, leaving me troubled.

Of course, I had heard the Good Friday story, and didn't like to think about it. Yet there it was, front and centre in the faith that was both puzzling and appealing to me at a young age. I was drawn to the stories Jesus told—so many felt encouraging, or challenging in ways that seemed like a legitimate part of growing up. Eventually I could deal with references to the cross, the agony of Jesus that made me feel anxious.

But I was never very successful in finding a satisfactory answer to the question, "Why?" Why was it so important, even 2000 years later? Why would Jesus have to die for the sins of the world or for my sins? What could that possibly mean for me, for us, today?

People are still killed in ugly ways; suffering for others is not exactly a unique pattern in history. What was conquered in the dying of Jesus on the cross, when human cruelty is still with us? Has anything really changed in the world because of the cross?

As I grew into adulthood, the questions grew as well. For example, if Jesus is dying to ransom us for our sins, who is being paid the ransom? Is the beneficiary Satan? Or God the Father? As questions mature, they become more uncomfortable, not less. I could not imagine sharing these questions with anybody who took the faith seriously. I was drawn to Jesus, yes, and found my life making more sense when I tried to put into practice what I thought I heard Him saying in the Bible. But I always had less confidence in the church and church leaders. Unanswered questions about the cross continued.

It didn't make sense to me that God needed to be paid with blood in order to relent and forgive wayward and stupid humans like me. When I heard the story Jesus told about the prodigal son, I quickly identified that Jesus didn't see the father of the prodigal son as requiring satisfaction before welcoming the wayward son. At all. If we who are so human forgive from love, not as payment, wouldn't God do the same, even more-so?

Through my knowing and not knowing, I identified as a Christian. I tried to trust Jesus, to follow Him. As an overly-introspective teen, I was afflicted for years with painful self-consciousness that made it hard for me even to talk with some people. My mind seemed to work ok, but I was convoluted internally in ways I couldn't express through my stutter.

It never would have occurred to me that Jesus might lead me out of that mental hall of mirrors. Rather, it seemed straightforward just to read the Bible once in a while, to talk to Jesus in prayer now and then, through uncertainties, doubts, failures, and loneliness, without clear answers to most questions. I persisted in attending church, even benefitting from what I considered a bad sermon by creating something better in my head as a passive-aggressive silent reaction.

If you had asked me what "the cross" meant, I would have said that it showed Jesus was fully human and identified with us. He suffered more than most of us ever will against the power of evil which is mysteriously also present in the world. If Jesus was the son of God living fully as a human, then it also meant he took our (my) humanity to the cross. The idea of the shepherd boy David killing Goliath to rescue his nation seemed to me the best ancient illustration of what Jesus did on the cross. Just as David's action benefited everyone in Israel, Jesus died—and then turned death inside out—for us all.

Eventually I read about theories of the atonement, which didn't really help my understanding. The words of the disciples—that Jesus died for us—I accepted without further explanation. There are many things in life we don't understand, but which we accept. I accepted the truth of Jesus giving up His life for the world, including me, without being able to articulate the nuances theologically the way some others seemed determined to do. Somehow, I felt that the death and resurrection broke the power of sin, and made forgiveness and the empowering presence of the Holy Spirit to help us to holiness available to everyone.

A major change for me came during a period of illness and crisis when a friend lent me a tape by the Franciscan priest Richard Rohr, targeted at Alcoholics Anonymous (AA) groups. One question, with its rhetorical answer, rose above everything else in that long talk. In me, it prompted a more challenging appreciation of the meaning of the cross, in humility, awe, and worship.

The question is: "What is the greatest human sin in history?" Take a few minutes to consider your answer. Review what you know, what you believe about good and evil, about human nature, about your own weaknesses and failures, about God.[15]

After a significant pause, the answer Rohr offered was, "When people killed Jesus, whom we believe is God in human form: wouldn't that be the most monstrous human sin?"

The second question: "What did God do with the sin of murdering the Son of God?"
Again, take a few moments to consider your own answer. What was God's reaction? Judgment? A heightened moral code? What resulted, spiritually, after Jesus' death?

Before answering that question, let's look at some history. In the 4th Century, Bishop Ambrose of Milan, who was instrumental in the conversion of St. Augustine, added a phrase to the developing liturgy of the early Christian church. This was before the split into Western Roman Catholic and Eastern Orthodox, and all the thousands of protestant splits since the Reformation. For over 1200 years, the most important worship service every year was the midnight worship on Holy Saturday. In focus was Jesus' cosmic breakthrough from death to life, between Good Friday and Easter Sunday. Crowds entered the dark church silently, just before midnight. One candle would be lit at the front, and there would be a series of readings that show the progression of God's engagement with the world leading to the coming of Jesus.

Then as the story of Jesus was told, a huge pan of oil would be set alight and everyone would begin shouting praises, making loud noise, and lighting candles, all signalling the miracle of the resurrection. At that moment, the Bishop stepped forward to lead a call-response pattern of prayer using older sentences, and inserting new insights, as loud as a cheerleader. We believe that Ambrose

---

[15] Ed. note: For more information, refer to Rohr's book *Breathing Under Water: Spirituality and the Twelve Steps* (Franciscan Media, 2011).

is the first one in history to add a startling phrase which is still present in the liturgy for Holy Saturday. In a long sequence of joyful prayers of praise, he said, "We praise you Lord God for *the Happy Sin* which brought about so great a redemption in Jesus." The phrase in Latin is "felix culpa" and it refers to the horror of Jesus' passion and death paradoxically resulting in salvation for the world.

So, what did God do with the greatest sin in history? Through it, He brought about the greatest redemption! The mysterious paradox central to God's heart for us conquers the sin of the world through the suffering and death of Jesus. His glorious resurrection from the dead expresses the mystery of God's intention in love for us, able to encompass the greatest sin, evil, and death with salvation, rescue, transformation, and life eternal in Christ!

Paradox is a "logically self-contradictory statement of opposites,"[16] which, contrary to expectations, works. The betrayal of Jesus, son of God, to death at the hands of humans—the greatest sin possible against God—is indeed a "felix culpa" (happy sin) if it led to the conquering of death for us, which it has. Jesus broke the power of Satan, of evil, and of death by fulfilling the faithfulness of his commitment to love us to the end. Spiritual powers that were always secondary to God, but rebellious, were decisively broken by the dying and rising of Jesus. Spiritual powers in our realm have shifted, with God's victory in Christ breaking into the light. The threat of death is now thrown down, the power of evil is broken, and all people are able to access the same power that raised Jesus from the dead, through actively trusting themselves to live in Christ, not simply in their own power.

As Paul says, God "is able to do above and beyond all that we ask or think according to *the power that works in us.*"[17] Christ's power is given

---

[16] https://en.wikipedia.org/wiki/Paradox
[17] Eph. 3:20

to work in us because the powers of evil have been disempowered; the age-old battle between God and Satan for control of humanity and creation has taken a decisive turn. It is clear to everyone, and to the cosmic powers themselves, who has won, is winning, and will win the battle. When we stand with Jesus, follow Jesus, confess and repent to Jesus, ask for strength and life and equipping to serve through Jesus, we are empowered in Him.

Jesus became one of us, incarnate (which literally means "enfleshed") to rescue all of us.[18] Look up some of the many references in the New Testament to "dying to your old self."[19] They call us to live in the paradox, with Jesus. As He accepted death on a cross and gave life to all who receive it from Him. We overcome the evil still fighting against us when we paradoxically live in the strength and weakness of Jesus, when we let go of ourselves, and lean fully into God's life in us through Christ. Through Jesus, our "suffering for righteousness' sake" is now a participation in Christ's rescue mission for all people, overturning evil through love, through the paradox. You could say I still don't understand it, but it gives me life. I now see the cross as the doorway from my old self to the new, from the old world to the new one, in Christ. Jesus dying and rising is central to what life is about for each of us, as God works to bring about the marriage of heaven and earth. My role is to try to be faithful, to speak honestly, to be myself, to follow Jesus through paradox to maturity. Maturity in Christ means joyful humility, not necessarily understanding everything; it means strength in weakness, Christ in us, the hope of glory; it means life in death, dying to ourselves and rising with Jesus day by day. The cross of Jesus is the turning point of history, the embrace of the prodigal Father, the entry into the paradox of God's grace and love in place of sin, rebellion, and death.

Praise to you, Lord Jesus Christ.

---

[18] Phil. 2:5-13
[19] Gal. 2:20, Rom. 6:11-14

Chapter 11

Confession
A Student has a Frightening Opportunity
by Ricky Lee

Ricky Lee is a worship leader and the executive director of Promise Vancouver. He is also the former director of operations for Journey Canada.

I once took a class taught by a teacher I revered. His lectures were an experience: illuminating, provocative, at times even mind-blowing. Sometimes they were also way over my head. I had a *lot* of questions but was too in awe of him to raise my hand (and too afraid of looking dumb). One day during a break a friend and I deliberated about something we had just heard in class. At one point she said, "That's a really great question. You should ask him." Not wanting to be seen as a coward I nodded and smiled big, as if to say, "Great idea!", while internally thinking, "Yeah right… that'll never happen!" But I was not prepared for what came next. My friend continued, "You can ask him now. He's right behind you!"

Confession can be a bit like that: a "now's your chance" moment, a very present opportunity. *Opportunity? For what?* For most of my life I didn't really know and frankly, didn't really care to find out. Truth be told, confession was something I never *really* intended to go through with. It seemed a little like the medieval medical practice of "bleeding"—archaic, painful, benefits questionable, probably leaving you worse off.

Every so often you hear news of someone turning themselves in, confessing to a crime. *What compels a person to do such a thing? To give up and accept the consequences?* My guess is it has something to do with scales tipping: *Run enough, you get tired. Hide enough, you run out of places. Guilt catches up, you get weighed down. Fear steals enough sleep, you get desperate.* At some point things add up and that "life of freedom" you're holding onto becomes not much of a life at all.

Enter *confession*. When we finally stop our running and hiding, when we put to rest our blaming and excuse-making, we arrive back at a place we've been avoiding all along. We're back at a "now's your chance" moment. Sometimes we call it a defining moment, or a divine appointment. Others call it "rock-bottom," and still others say "grace." Whatever you call it—and whether confessing to a heinous crime, hurtful words, or spilled milk—I have learned that confession is essentially the same thing, every time: *letting Truth do its thing.*

Confession is our chance to tell the whole truth, the real truth. And whether we realize it or not, when we get really honest, we are being *authentic*, a risky and scary business, but with a real upside, too. In telling the truth we arrive at a place of rest—we get a break from the tiring dance of half-truths, lies, and keeping up appearances... this kind of a break can feel like a vacation (which can be really nice!).

Like a vacation, it's better when you take someone along. Confessing to a real life, flesh-and-blood human is scary, at first. For most it's nauseating to tell someone your darkest secrets. Here we face intense temptation to divert the conversation, or just give the diet version, or set the building on fire. But we must stay the course to let truth be true. Maybe harder are those moments immediately after "spilling the beans." *Wincing, we wait for the blow. Their verdict. Horror? Disgust? Rejection?* But let's just imagine this: what if they hear you, *and* still want to hang around? *Wow, mercy.*

Like any vacation, who accompanies you is important. The wrong companion can ruin a good experience. *So, who to bring along?* A safe bet would be someone who has been where you are and a little beyond. Someone who has tasted that *"Wow, mercy."* Someone who *knows* that confession is about truth encountering mercy.

One quick note about truth: it gets a bad rap as being cold and merciless. Excuse the pun, but that couldn't be farther from *the truth*. What's not to like about truth if it *sets us free*? Isn't it good to *cut through the crap* so you can get on with the real good stuff? Every confession begins by just *telling it like it is*, but that's just the beginning because in *true* confession we don't just tell the truth, we encounter the *Truth*.

And here we get to the *real* good news about confession. When we finally face the Truth, surprise! Truth isn't an abstract idea or a set of morals and laws. Instead, we discover *Truth is a person*. Not cold and merciless, but *good*, through and through. Truth already knows your name, has heard the cries of your heart, and no matter what awful thing you might bring to confession, Truth is unphased and prepared to accept you, take you back, and love you with a love that outweighs anything you've ever done, or has been done to you.

Put another way, each time we confess is another moment to hear the Good News, another chance to "believe." Truth *does its thing* and we find ourselves reliving the Gospel story—light breaks into our darkness, and what was dark is now light. We die to ourselves, but then return to what we were born for: *living*. In confession we are "born again," *again*.

So, the next time you're given the chance to confess, do it and let Truth do its thing.

Chapter 12

A Husband and Wife Learn they are Safe
by Raena and Karl Peters

Raena and Karl Peters are parents living in Winnipeg, Manitoba where Raena is a Journey program coordinator.

Karl—Like many people, I want a quick fix. Theoretically in a conversation I would acknowledge that a quick fix is not the best path forward. But my actions can communicate the contrary.

We live in an old house, in need of many repairs and renovations. Slapping a coat of paint on our hallway may improve things at first glance but if we do not take the time to properly prepare the wall for painting, washing it and cleaning up chipped and peeling paint, the finished product won't look very good on a close inspection. If we don't patch the plaster holes or level out the bumps, it's going to look like a cheap job. But to get into the nitty gritty of the job is overwhelming. What if we start prepping the wall and the paint starts chipping and peeling more and more? Or chunks of old plaster start falling off? I avoid getting close to the work for fear the work is even more than what meets the eye.

When we don't have large chunks of time to put towards a project, our tendency is to avoid the project altogether. Both Raena and I tend to be all-or-nothing in the way we approach things.
We could take a small amount of time to work on the chipping paint one weekend, and then work on tending to the plaster on another, all the while working towards that beautiful final coat of paint that

will be an enjoyable finished product. Instead, we sit around waiting for the time and energy to descend upon us to do the whole thing at once. But with three kids under the age of six, that is likely not going to present itself!

I also want quick fixes in my relationships. I want the enjoyment of friendships, in my relationship with Raena, and even with my kids without the more difficult and more detailed work of being vulnerable, working through conflict, and challenging myself to step out of my comfort zone and view situations from the perspectives, experiences, and feelings of others. This spills over into my relationship with God the Father as well. I would like to come to the Father and receive all that He promises me instantaneously. But God our Father doesn't want to just slap a cheap coat of paint over my life to make it look pretty on the outside. He wants to do quality work with the whole of who I am. If I take the quick approach with opening myself up to the Father's loving presence, I may get a small taste of what I am looking for, but generally overtime I am disappointed with the overall outcome. The chipped paint and bumps in the plaster start to show through the top coat of paint I was hoping would freshen everything up. To experience the depths of love He offers me, I have to be willing to do the more nitty-gritty work of opening up my whole heart.

Raena—My father had his own life story before I came along. We become a part of the stories our parents are already living, no matter their aches, to make something new for us. New things can be birthed but are still intertwined with the stories of the past. For all of my dad's own pain and shortcomings, he pointed me towards the love of a Father far greater than he. My image of Him was interrupted and blocked along the way. By the pain and suffering of my own father but also by the pain and suffering of the world.

Karl—My mom died when I was twelve and, shortly after, my father had serious health issues which left him stuck in bed for hours of the day. During my teenage years, my brothers and I spent much of our time on our own. As I grew up, I found myself feeling lost and unsure of my place in the world around me.

I often struggle to feel God is near and that He actually cares about me. I feel I need to do more, be more, to be noticed by God. I feel as though nothing I do is ever good enough for God. I am always failing, and more trouble to God than anything else. It makes no difference to God if I spend time with Him or not.

I imagine Jesus as the nice one, and God is the serious, harsh one. When I think about it, I know these beliefs of mine are false. Throughout the Bible, God demonstrates His deep love and care for His people. He demonstrates His loyalty and commitment to His children, even when they are wandering, stubborn, and rebellious.

Raena—Growing up I often felt alone and lost, wondering who I was and where I fit in this world. My dad was there for me in a lot of good ways, but he was also on his own journey of seeking the answers to these questions for himself. I emerged out of childhood and into young adulthood, presenting well on the outside in a lot of ways but internally struggling with self-confidence and floundering in a sense of my identity and direction in life. In some sense this is the natural journey of young adulthood, discovering who we are more fully and how we fit into the collective human experience in a meaningful and life-giving way. But many of my insecurities ran deep, and my lack of direction was incapacitating at times. I didn't have the confidence and skills I needed to relate to others and myself in the healthy and life-giving way I craved. I needed someone to name me and affirm me and help me keep taking the next step forward.

For all the agency we have in our own lives, we can't control the history we are born into and the lived reality of our families. How do we experience the goodness of the Father when our own fathers are, at best, a mere glimpse of the fullness of all that He is?
The journey to know the Father can be a long and painful one—the road less traveled in this world of sorrows. How does one expose

one's heart to further risk? A love that may be a mirage. A love that seems to represent something more like a fairy tale. Love is a hope we want our children to hold on to and not let go of as they grow old, but we lose love along the way. Bits of our heart are left behind. Marred, broken, and stained—how do we open our hearts up to healing and redeeming love?

We all yearn to experience perfect love. And most of us can relate to the longings for a perfect father. We have experienced many broken expressions of fatherhood in this hurting world. Where do we turn when even a healthy father, a good father, can not meet all the aches inside of us and longing to be fully loved and connected to something bigger than ourselves. Ideally, our experience of father would include an expression of generous, selfless love, one where we can catch a glimpse of what our heavenly Father is like so that we can connect to Him more easily. How do we connect to the Father when our understanding of Him is so weak? And our hearts are so broken from the pain and suffering in this world?

I was very uncomfortable in my own skin, so it has taken time for me to feel comfortable sitting with the Father and allowing Him to be present to me. Accepting the way He affirms me and names me has been a process of building small amounts of trust over time that has led to a relationship that now feels more tangible. At first, it was more head knowledge, whereas now I can sense it in more of my whole person, body, mind, heart, and soul. I used to read or learn something and it would make sense to me, but I would have a lot of trouble integrating what I knew into my everyday life situations.

As I have opened my heart up to Father God, He has named me! He has called me to discover more of who I am and empowered me to persevere. As we consistently sit with Him in the silence and pain of life, He sits with us and beckons us forward to take the next step. Sometimes the step flows naturally and feels simple and freeing, sometimes it is painful and arduous, and sometimes it feels like we are stepping into an abyss. But as we continue to consistently accept His invitation of love, as we allow Him to name us, and empower us, we build trust over time and grow in our sense of safety in His presence.

Even now, it can take a conscious effort not to fight off the affirmations I am longing for. When I open up my heart to His help, He is there to empower me to persevere and brings people into my life to help me along the way. Through opening myself up to something deeper than a quick fix, I have experienced the more thorough job of restoring a broken-down house. Not all the rooms of my heart have gone through renovation and restoration, but I can persevere to begin working on the next room with a loving and safe Father because He has shown His faithfulness to me in everything He has restored thus far.

Karl—Learning to trust God as my Father has taken time. It has been uncomfortable at times as I let my guard down. A father is meant to guide, teach, direct, discipline, encourage, and name. A father prepares the child to explore the world with confidence. They are secure, knowing their place in the world. Knowing that they are important. As I have allowed the Father in, I learn more about His character and trustworthiness. I know God cares for me. Although I often struggle with believing otherwise, I know that God calls me his child. I am His. He has named me and cheers me on when I take on new things. As a dad to three girls, I am so proud to see them grow, learn, and face their fears. The feelings of pride and joy that I have while watching them grow sometimes overwhelms me. It is in moments like those that I remember that I am God's child. God feels the same way about me.

When our oldest first learned to ride her bike on a road, she had to practice moving to the side of the road when cars passed. I saw her do this without a reminder and told her I felt good to know she was being safe. She responded by saying, "And you are proud of me." It was not a question. She *knew* I was proud of her. It is a good reminder of how my Father sees me.

Chapter 13

The Wisdom of Accepted Tenderness
by Dorothy Bingen

*D*orothy *Bingen is a pastor and mediator. She is a long-time Journey leader.*

> I have calmed and quieted my soul
> like a weaned child with its mother;
> my soul is like a weaned child.

-Psalm 131:2

In this verse, David appeals to our earliest and most tender memories, reminding us of the safety and warmth we found in our mother's arms. We are vulnerable and finite people, but we are invited to find our rest and refuge in God; we are invited to rest contentedly with the God of hope. The warrior king of Israel, who knew his own vulnerabilities and limitations, parallels his experience of resting in God to a child lying contentedly on her mother.

I find it difficult to identify or connect with David's words. Although I have both memories and pictures of myself as a young child leaning contentedly on my father's chest, I have found no such pictures with my mother, either in a photo album or in my imagination.

I am a daughter from three generations of mothers whose mothering was disrupted by untimely death, abuse, and trauma. My great-grandmother died after childbirth when my grandmother was 7, and so was completely absent. She was followed by her daughter and granddaughter, whose trauma made them emotionally absent mothers. As a child, I sensed that the only chance I had to receive love from my mother was to never make a mistake and to excel in all that I did. I entered adulthood being hard on myself and others. I barely knew what comfort, warmth, and empathy felt like. I walled myself off from any emotions that made me feel vulnerable, like sadness, loneliness, and grief.

As I encountered the Holy Spirit in university, a thaw began. I began to feel sadness and loss. At 27, I became a mother and this sadness intensified. I felt empty inside. As I held my son and sang to him and laughed with him, I longed for this same kind of mother love to be directed towards me. But there was just emptiness. God felt far away, and no matter how hard I tried to open myself up to God's love, I imagined God required perfection and expected me to work tirelessly on God's behalf. Years went by, I had two more children and still there was knowledge of this emptiness, this inability to rest in God's goodness and love, and a deep grief that accompanied it.

I was invited to attend a week-long Journey Intensive retreat at Harrison Hot Springs in the summer of 1995. I brought my third child with me—a contented baby girl who delighted in all the attention she got. That year a team from New Zealand joined us and we loved their enthusiasm and joy.

In those days, neither Journey nor the church taught much about the role of a mothering God and I felt very stuck as to how to process my grief. One day during worship I found myself deeply feeling the absence of a mother's love, and I was crying out to God to meet me in this place. A Māori woman named Donna came up to me and asked if she could pray for me. She was a warm and generous person with a contagious laugh. She gently prayed for me and, as she did, she enveloped me in her arms. At that moment God began to reveal a mother's love to me. This love was soft and warm and tender. I was assured of God's love for me, no need for perfection and performance. Warmth flowed through me and I sensed a letting go within me, an ability to rest in God's arms, like a weaned child with her mother.

I continue to encounter God's mothering love through prayer and through reading and meditating on the Scriptures. This has included verses like Psalm 27:10, where David writes, "Even if my father and mother abandon me, the LORD cares for me." How delightful to be received by God, the one who parents us! I can picture God, the midwife, joyfully receiving us, even when we are forsaken.

Another such passage is Isaiah 49, in which Zion accuses the Lord of forsaking and forgetting them. The Lord responds to this charge: "Can a woman forget her nursing child, or lack compassion (rhm) for the child of her womb? Even if these forget, yet I will not forget you."[20] The word "compassion" [מחרם (rhm)] is often translated as mercy or tenderness and comes from the root of a word for womb. "Compassion" is used to describe God's love 26 times in Scripture, often in combination with Hesed (God's faithful love). God's love is a womb-like love; God loves us with the tenderness and compassion of a mother.

God's mothering love has also been revealed to me through a combination of Jesus' parable of the lost coin and the example of my mother-in-law, Ruth. Ruth has lived with us for 20 years and she is always available to help. We particularly call upon her when we have lost something; Ruth will sweep and dig under piles and look until what was lost is found. In Luke 15, Jesus uses a story of such a woman to describe God's love—looking for a lost coin and

---

[20] Isa. 49:15

delighting when it is found. God is like a woman who sweeps and uncovers; God's love is yearning, searching, and inclusive.

Experiencing God's mothering love in the midst of my emptiness has been transformational for me. I have been welcomed with open arms by the one who is always ready to receive me. This love has enabled me to let go of my expectation that my mother meets a need within me that only God can meet. Experiencing God's mother-love has enabled me to continue to face pain in my life and to receive comfort. And I pray for God to enable me to extend compassion and care for those who cross my path.

> And you, Jesus, are you not also a mother?
> Are you not the mother who, like a hen,
> gathers her chickens under her wings?
> Truly, Lord, you are a mother;
> for both they who are in labour
> and they who are brought forth
> are accepted by you.

> -St. Anselm (1033-1109)

Chapter 14

Throwing Ourselves into God
by Jeff Hayashi

Jeff Hayashi is a therapist and spiritual director based out of Vancouver. He and his wife, Brenda, have been friends of Journey from its earliest days.

A life fully lived is a life lived from the heart.

There is something potent and irrepressible inside the human spirit that drives each one of us toward living a whole-hearted life. How amazing it is that this fiery spark within is a direct expression of our being made in the image of God, the Whole One, who is ever-drawing us back into His own heart, where our wholeness resides.

As persons created in the image of One so extraordinary, we too are wondrous and multi-faceted beings. This means that, despite all of the traumatic wounds and soul-fractures we sustain in this life, even our lost parts are God-imprinted to move us back toward realignment. Perhaps the most universal rupture inside of us as human beings is the split between the head and the heart. In some, this split is a fissure, in others a chasm, in others still, a continental divide. No matter the degree, this breach exists within us all, and we are always reaching to be reunited within ourselves. How can these two essential worlds be bridged?

Thankfully, we can draw much help from ancient wisdom. The early Christian fathers and mothers from centuries ago have passed down a key through the ages that has safely arrived in our hands today. That key is this: the knowledge of God by way of the mind is always in service to the *knowing* that comes by way of the *heart*. None of these forebearers would deny the vitality and necessity of the mind in the pursuit of God, but they emphasize the need to move from "mere knowledge" to something more transcendent. The shift from a Greek-informed "way of knowledge" to a Hebraic "way of knowing" moves us from grasping for God through "thinking" into something far bigger and wilder—actively encountering God through love.

The mind, which is used to being in control, cannot force its way into this encounter. It desperately wants to and can be very insistent in trying! But while the mind can faithfully lead us to the door, this doorway into love requires the yielding of *trust* to turn the handle and lead us inside.

We see this movement unfolding in the perplexing prayer from Ephesians, where Paul prays that we would "*know* Christ's love that *surpasses knowledge.*"[21] It presents as a contradictory enigma at first: how do we know something beyond knowing? Yet both the mystery and the answer are held within that single line: "the way of knowing which transcends knowledge" is linked to an encounter with love. This is a "knowing by heart," where love gets inside of us in a way that changes everything. It is the difference between reading about someone we've long admired only to now sit face-to-face with them, listening in shock to the plot-twist as this person celebrates *us* with unbridled exuberance! When living by heart, we're no longer simply reading the story about God's love, rather we've entered into the folds of the pages and become a main character in it, fully a part and inked in.

Regarding this movement, one of the most striking illustrations that I've ever heard was relayed by Toni Dolfo-Smith many years ago following his visit to an art gallery in France. Toni described his

---

[21] Eph. 3:19

experience of coming across a replica of Rodin's famous bronzed statue "The Thinker"—the larger-than-life masterpiece of a man sitting in deep reflection. The artist had skillfully recaptured and re-rendered this work not from bronze but from a transparent Lucite substance. The clarity of this substance allowed a direct line of sight into a dynamic, colourful cluster of wires constituting the Thinker's brain which then freely cascaded down through his neck to then regather in his chest. There it clustered into another colourful matrix constituting the Thinker's heart. What a striking work of art.

It wasn't until Toni took a closer step forward and examined the piece more carefully that he noticed that midway between the head and the heart, an entire cross-section of wiring had been cut clean through and surgically extracted from the continuum. Despite what appeared at first glance to be a vibrant confluence of connectivity, the lines had been breached, the connection severed. This "split," while almost imperceptible, was, in fact, absolute and intractable. The thinker was actually "trapped in his thinking" while artfully portraying the illusion of a more vivid, integrated life.

This modern artist captured something that speaks universally. If this disconnection of pathways is so short-circuiting of the true vitality that we all long for, why then is this internal breach something that we all tend toward? Looking within, we can easily spot two fear-instincts that are at work. Both of these instincts are more reflexive and run counter to that deeper impulse within that compels us toward wholeness.

The first instinct is that *we fear our own hearts*. We sense a wildness and unpredictability at the depths within us. Like the darkening of the sea the deeper we go down, the scarier and more pressurized it gets. We instinctively know there is treasure at the bottom but we sense the swarm and swirl of other daunting creatures which surround these troves. Our internal sonar picks up on obscure sounds signalling deep hurts, unmet longings, unruly appetites, stinging disappointments, and confusions that lurk below.

The murkiness of our hearts provokes us to keep us closer to the surface, where more natural light flashes through and where we can manoeuvre by our senses. However, the churning of these other forces continues sounding forth from below.

A great courage is required to "go there" and face these parts of ourselves to bring light *to* them so that healing and integration can happen. Courage is fitting, as the word itself is derived from the Latin "cor" which means "heart." That is, we need courage of heart to face into our hearts. We never need to plumb these depths alone. The Holy Spirit, the En-courager, comes alongside to give us courage by giving of His own presence of heart. The Psalmist understood and exercised this courage in his deep prayer to Yahweh: "Search me, O God, and know my heart... See if there be any wicked way in me, and lead me in the way everlasting."[22] We see him risk trusting love over fear out of his desire to know and be known.

The second instinct that splits us off from within is that *we fear God's heart*. Perhaps closer to home, we fear that God is *"heartless."* This fear broadcasts its frequency to our minds and crosses signals with the truth that God dwells in absolute perfection and purity. So while this instinct touches the truth—God is holy—fear then distorts Yahweh's divine "otherness" into divine aloofness. Now, rather than risking the release of our own hearts into such a Heart, we draw back. We wonder how could the One who "is light" in whom there is "absolutely no darkness"[23] look upon us deeply flawed creatures with any tender affections at all?

What we have done here is we have taken our own "artistic license" to sculpt God into our own image—now *God* has become The Thinker, hunched over on himself, poised in a cerebral, inanimate, emotionless state. We forcibly project into Him our own internal

[22] Ps. 139:23-24 KJV
[23] 1 John 1:5

breach of head and heart, segregating His perfection from His affections. How can there be warmth toward us when the lines within Him are cut? We sever and extract from Him the very friendship that defines Him. We tend to see Him sitting solo, in isolation, devoid of any trinitarian dance or relational joy, fixed into cold bronze, hard-wired not to feel. Perhaps these wires spark now and again with a faint flicker of emotion here or there. Yet, by and large, He looks down from His elevated vantage point to "think thoughts" about us, ponderings that emanate from an etched-in furrow at His brow.

But the truth is there is no breach in God. None. There is, in fact, an energetic harmony, all cylinders firing, between the divine mind and heart. Perfect genius ignited by perfect love, totally aligned, casting out fear. This energized unity is both within and without, meaning our God is also thriving in a dynamic friendship between the three persons of the divine community. They live in explosive joy saturated in perfect peace. The life inside that friendship is *so* alive that it energizes all the stars, suns and galaxies in the universe along with every human heartbeat. Yes, beneath each beating heart is God's own heart of affection toward that person, His "I love you," the very beating pulse of each one of us. All life flows from this love! Here we can translate "God is love" to "God is an open heart." This is the Heart that is ever-moving toward us to secure our identities in love.

When we're so secured, we move from seeing God's purity as merely His morality, like a matrix of trip-wires within His chest and head that we might set off with our many missteps. No, we now experience God's *holiness* as a direct outflow of His *"whole-liness,"* from the perfect relational harmony that defines His being. In other words, even the holiness of God flows from His love. We can begin to let go and trust that our hearts which long to be received will not only be received but fully embraced into His abounding affection.

That is why the call of discipleship is neither to think our way to God, nor to moralize our way in. In fact, it is more than this, not less: it is to hurl our entire hearts into His heart, trusting that He not only will meet us *with* love... but that He *IS* love. Out of His own wholeness that Love is shouting a hearty "YES!" over us. The more "rooted and established in this love"[24] we are, the more we find the courage of self-abandonment, and in so doing, find Him.

This love moved Him to extraordinary lengths to show us that He can be trusted this whole-heartedly. The stone-stoic god we've cast in bronze is a myth of our own making. The real God stepped forward and stepped into skin so that He could breathe and bleed like us. His incarnation translates to "I am an open heart!" Total access given. We can now take heart and dare delve into the depths of His loving kindness. This *is* the "deep calling to deep" of the Psalms. This is the call of Love and it has always been and will always be, Heart to heart.

---

[24] Eph: 3:17

Chapter 15

The Truth
Knowing who we Truly Are
by Jeff Cottam

Jeff Cottam is an amateur baker and chef currently perfecting his French baguette. He has worked with Journey as a volunteer for 10 years.

Who are you when you are with other people? Kind of a funny question to ask I suppose. You might quickly respond by saying "I'm me." However, take a moment, and think about it. Is it possible that you have different versions of yourself for different people? In varying degrees, I believe this is something we all struggle with.

I have a cousin named Derek who is thirteen years my senior. When I was young, I thought he was so cool. He had a cool job in advertising, cool style, and cool demeanor—cool. When we would have family gatherings, I would spend a good amount of time obsessing about what I was going to wear to impress him. My younger brother saw right through me and knew exactly what I was doing. "You're trying to be cool for Derek, aren't you?" I can laugh now but back then the stakes were high and I meant business.

I can remember a couple times when my cousin complimented me, and I would respond so nonchalantly, "Oh thanks," as if I didn't change fifteen times before deciding on the outfit. Meanwhile I was doing the Cha Cha inside, shouting, "HE THINKS I AM COOL!" What I was really shouting was, "I am ACCEPTED!" That happiness lasted for the night but, the next day, the feelings of acceptance were gone, and I was at school where I was wearing a good boy mask,

seeking praise from my teachers, parents, and peers. What a joyous occasion it was when I would receive affirmation and accolades. For me, the hard work was with the hope that I would hear, "Great job, you're amazing." These behaviours and their consequent responses laid a very shaky foundation for authentic relationships as my personal sense of value and self-worth was bound by the lie that I need to perform or present myself in a certain way to be accepted.

To clarify—it is Godly to perform with excellence. In fact, the Bible instructs us to do everything well. For example, the Word says that the prophet Daniel had a spirit of excellence in him. Where I believe we get it wrong is allowing our identity to be built and informed by what we do, not who we are in Jesus. These masks of performance or, "I'm fine. Everything's great," become very heavy to hold, yet we find them so incredibly hard to lay down. But that is exactly what Jesus is inviting us to do. Jesus wants to see you! Yes you, the real you, and he wants others to see you too. What does this mean, "the real me"? It means all of you—the good, the bad, and the "I can't believe I did that."

So often the shame of our mistakes and failures leads us to want to hide from other people. If the enemy can keep us in this place of isolation, we will miss out on so much life. I am not telling you to stop traffic on a Sunday morning and tell the greeter all your trials and woes, but Jesus is asking you to find trusted brothers and sisters in the body of Christ that you can begin to walk with. But man, that can be scary! What would people think if they knew what was really going on in my life?

Aside from my fear, I also believed a lie that no one who would want to walk with me and be committed to me, because if they knew the real stuff it would be too much. This is just not true. There are people who want to walk with you, baggage and all.

I can remember the first person I told some of my struggles to. I am not sure how I was expecting him to react, but a kind smile came across his face. I felt no condemnation, no judgement and no shame. He met me with love, acceptance, and gratitude. He said, "Thank you." This step of faith was the first time where I was alive in the real me. Had I not had that conversation, I am not so sure I would be writing to you today.

In my journey some of the moments where I have felt most close to Jesus are the ones that have been spent in the company of friends and believers that I have chosen to walk with. The moments where I confess sin, reveal a struggle, or even a frustration are the moments where I am led to the cross by fellow sinners, and I experience the love and embrace of Jesus. Sometimes I am being led to the cross and sometimes I am leading, but the truth is we all benefit as we watch Jesus faithfully minister to His beloved.

The false self and the masks we choose to live behind keep us separated from Jesus as we build an identity that is not rooted in Him. Jesus wants to walk with us. For some reason, many Christians have a hard time believing this in their heart. Not only this, but we fear what we will have to give up. Fear not; what you have to gain far outweighs what you hand over to Him. Jesus is a gentleman. He knows when you are ready and He walks with us by our side.

As you continue to walk with Jesus and the body of Christ, you will begin to live from a place of knowing you are deeply loved, and your true self will be free to be expressed. You will be secure and not have to change 15 times before meeting your cousin. You will know that your identity is not based on your ability to perform, but most importantly, when you stand firm in your true self, you will be able to extend that same authentic love to others.

Section 3—Coming Home

One of the dangers of the metaphor of the journey for the spiritual life is that we could easily think that there is an endpoint—that there is a moment when we grow past having needs, or having to continue to walk the path. However, we will always need Jesus, we will never mature past our dependence on Him. As humans, we always need love, always need a sense of significance—these are not things that we grow out of. Additionally, the wounds we have suffered in this life will not disappear—there are always scars. Our spiritual and emotional wounds work a lot like physical wounds, the injury may have some healing, but there are often consequences that endure.

And so, even though we've called this section "Coming Home" there is a sense in which we will never truly come home until Jesus comes back. This should not discourage us—we can still make progress and live into greater joy and creativity, but that ability will be rooted in dependence on God. Our journey is, in many ways, an exploration of His sufficiency—learning more and more how much He loves us, how much attention He is willing to lavish on us, of the ways He is reconciling all things into Christ Jesus.

One of the paradoxes of the Christian life is that exploring the love of God is not always easy or pleasant. When God says that He is sufficient, He is also saying that other things are not. This means that His invitation is, very often, to step away from the things that we think we need and to turn in simplicity to Him.

I am writing this on a morning in which I woke up discouraged. There has been a lot going on in this year of pandemic—we have lost family to death and illness and we have not been able to mourn the way we could have before COVID-19. To top it off, I blew out a tire on my car just a couple of hours ago, and I'm worried about the cost to repair it. I find myself questioning the goodness of God, which is not something a spiritual, full-time minister is supposed to be thinking. When I opened my email, I found David Gotts' remarkable meditation on weakness and strength in Christ (chapter 18, *Strength*). I find that the love of God is stern stuff—I am called to die to myself. The good news, the gospel, is that I will find new life in Him.

> *"Everyone who lives and believes in me will never die. Do you believe this?"*

> *-John 11:26*

> *-GL*

"A Walk in the Park" by Kathleen Morrissey - Photograph

A Prodigal Son

Does that lamp still burn in my Father's house,
Which he kindled the night I went away?
I turned once beneath the cedar boughs,
And marked it gleam with a golden ray;
Did he think to light me home some day?

Hungry here with the crunching swine,
Hungry harvest have I to reap;
In a dream I count my Father's kine,
I hear the tinkling bells of his sheep,
I watch his lambs that browse and leap.

There is plenty of bread at home,
His servants have bread enough and to spare;
The purple wine-fat froths with foam,
Oil and spices make sweet the air,
While I perish hungry and bare.

Rich and blessed those servants, rather
Than I who see not my Father's face!
I will arise and go to my Father: -
"Fallen from sonship, beggared of grace,
Grant me, Father, a servant's place."

- Christina Rossetti

Chapter 16

Understanding What Makes Me Tick
by Paul Kane

Paul Kane lives in Burnaby, BC where he works as a teacher. He was a participant in the Journey program in 2013.

The heart is an interesting machine. I'm not referring to the blood-pumper in our chest, but to that distinct part of us that is involved in decision taking, love making, and relationship managing. Like many of the machines in our life, we go about our day unconscious of its existence and operation—that is, until it breaks down. Suddenly, we become keenly aware of our heart! In that moment (or perhaps after a long process), we realize that the way our heart is functioning isn't helpful and a change is required.

One significant heart breakdown of mine happened just a few years ago, but it was a long time coming. Growing up, I was always aware that something wasn't quite right with how my heart-machine ran. Relating to my male peers was always a challenge—everything seemed to be a competition and I could never win. To soothe my regularly-bruised ego, I turned to elitism, valuing brains over brawn, snide remarks over supportive ones. But that further aggravated my isolation. As I became less and less desirable as a friend, the message played over and over in my mind: "You're not good enough!" I, of course, wasn't aware of what was causing the trail of blue smoke behind me as I went whizzing down the highway of life. I could smell the burning oil but didn't think I could do anything about it.

Coincidentally, my first car had a problem with burning oil (still does, my father reports). But once we realized that the damage to the piston rings in the engine would cost more to fix than the car itself was worth, my dad and I just put in special high-mileage oil and prayed things wouldn't get worse. It's still running today!

I, on the other hand, ran my little heart-machine into the ground. You see, relating to my male peers was further complicated by the fact that when it came to sexuality, I was (and am!) mostly attracted to men. Oddly enough, I was never particularly attracted to men romantically. This was quite convenient, especially in light of my choice to hold to the traditional Christian understanding of sex and marriage. While figuring out what it meant to be a Christian and a sexual being was still a challenge, eventually I came to peace with the facts of my life: I was attracted to men, was loved by God, and would remain single.

Most people, religious or not, cannot accept these facts about me. They might say, "You need to date men!" or "You need to find a wife!" but mostly, they say "How will you find love?" The last question is the true question, and it was the question I was asking myself. Love was the gasoline I ran on and my tank always felt almost empty. But I knew I'd never find love—romantic love— with a man.

Until the day I did.

I say I found love, but I actually mean I *fell* in love which is not at all the same thing. In fact, falling in love made the almost-empty feeling in my love-tank feel even emptier. This was mostly because the man I fell in love with did not return my love. I met Mr. Embers (so nicknamed because there was a teeny tiny burning in my heart for him) through some church events and I quickly admired him. He was well spoken, kind, and good looking. He also had a keen spiritual awareness and a pastoral heart, so I often found myself drawn to God through his words.

At first, I just wanted to be his friend, but as he gave me *a little* attention, my attraction grew. I started thinking about him when my mind wasn't occupied. I would check my phone often to see if he had returned my texts. Throughout the day, I would create little plans for ways to connect with him, to impress him. And behind all that, one question kept replaying in my mind: "Do I matter to Embers?" As this dragged on, I had to slowly and reluctantly admit to myself that I had fallen in love. And yet, I knew that this man who was "pleasing to the eye, and also desirable for gaining wisdom" was not for me.

What made matters worse was that I didn't feel I could share my situation with anyone. So much personal information would have to be shared and the shame of it was overwhelming. So, I stayed silent and my mind continued its course with ever-increasing revolutions per minute. Eventually though, it became so exhausting to be "in love" that I had to tell someone. I called up a long-time mentor who knew about my sexuality and, with many tears, explained my tale of woe. His kindness and encouragement met me where I was in that moment and he validated my pain. That being said, he also warned me that a journey was ahead of me, a heart journey of unknown length and route, but that God would be a trustworthy navigator through it all.

Okay, I don't journal. But for some odd reason, the next morning I started to write down my thoughts—and I'm so glad I did! Looking back now, I see how God, in His mercy and grace, used the following years to increase my awareness of my broken heart-machine and to slowly, piece by piece, part by part, take it apart, replace damaged bits, and then put it back together again.

One thing in particular that God showed me in that time was my damaged self-image. A few months after the phone call with my mentor, I started a series of counseling sessions. Like anyone who knows even a little about how the human heart *should* function, my counselor brought my attention to some self-hate I was harboring.

In my sessions, I had shared about my childhood self, the little boy who was desperate to connect with his male peers and had many times been hurt by them. I told one specific story of hurt to my counselor who proceeded to ask what Jesus would have said to hurting little-me to comfort him. I couldn't answer. I couldn't even say what adult-me would say!

It wasn't until a few days later, in prayer, as I reflected on that story, that the extent of my self-hate became clear to me. I loathed the awkward little boy who was being rejected by his peers. I hated the boy who thought he was better than everyone else but clearly was not. How idiotic he was to think he'd win friends by being mean.

And yet, he was a child.

Suddenly, the irony hit me: how was it that I, who work as an elementary school teacher, when presented with a hurting child, couldn't find words of comfort for him?! Tears streamed down my adult face as I confessed my self-hatred to God. I had for so long been depriving myself of love from the one flesh-and-blood person who was always with me: myself.

From there, God started revealing to me who I really am and who He made me to be. I quickly fell in love with the little kid who was me, with all his quirks and awkwardness but also his gifts and sensitivities. He was someone God loved and someone God had plans for.

It turned out to be a monumental shift. I started to realize in the coming year that part of why I so desperately wanted Embers to love me was because I had been seeking validation for who I was. I had been so love-empty that I tried to get it from someone who I thought could provide. And yet, Embers could not even come close to giving me the love I needed. In fact, the more God showed His love for me, the more I realized that no one would be able to match what He offered.

Armed with this diagnosis of my situation, I realized I had never truly been "in love" with Mr. Embers. True love wasn't needy in that way. Rather, the feelings I had for him had just been a symptom of my empty love-tank. Now that I knew what I was feeling, I could stop investing so much mental energy into trying to win Ember's love, and spend it instead on learning to love and be loved by God. The result was intensely liberating! I had no idea how much I had been spinning my wheels. But now, I was moving forward once again and the sensation was exhilarating.

In hindsight, I see that it took a breakdown to realize there was a problem with my heart-machine. It also took some expert help for me to realize what the problem was. But ultimately, it was God who put in the work to fix my broken heart.

Sometimes, I wonder why God doesn't just trade me in for a better model. Things are improving, but in so many ways, I'm still a lemon. Why does he spend so much time investing in me? But as I grow in knowledge of who He is and how He sees me, I'm starting to get it. To God, I'm a priceless collector's item. There's still so much to learn about what that means, but the thought of it, the thought of the journey of unknown length and route is becoming more and more enjoyable as I get to know and fall deeper in love with the One who made me and who is with me on the journey.

Chapter 17

Practicing Curiosity and Compassion
by Andrea Heavenor

Andrea Heavenor is a Vancouver nurse and artist. She works with Journey providing support and prayer for women affected by sexual abuse and sexual addiction.

I am not sure when I first felt the need to put on the "I'm fine" face. Somehow, I had learned that keeping silent meant "we're not going there" and unpleasant emotions were not welcome. Stuffing down my emotions and staying silent became my friends. Because of early trauma, I hated my body, and struggled with thoughts of self-harm and shame. The early protectors for my wounded heart were control, perfectionism, being a good girl, an eating disorder and an exercise addiction.

> Then Jesus told them to give her something to eat.
> Her parents were astonished, but he ordered them
> not to tell anyone what had happened.
>
> -Luke 8: 55-56 NIV

The gospel of Luke records Jesus' words after He raised Jairus' daughter from the dead. These instructions demonstrate that Jesus was more interested in caring for the girl than letting the crowd that was mourning outside know what He had done. With His request to feed her, Jesus was prioritizing the importance of nurturing, attending to and caring for new life. This caring of new life is a way of protection.

Choosing a New Protection

In our childhood, many of us adopt behaviors to soothe or hide our emotional pain. Examples of early protective behaviors are addictions, lying, denial, control, perfectionism and being the good girl/boy. These protectors work hard to keep us from feeling any unpleasant emotions like shame, fear, self-contempt, and guilt.

Jesus desires to care for our wounded hearts and free us from these unhealthy protective behaviours. He invites us to lay these down and give Him access to our hearts. As we respond to His invitation, He begins to transform us and, as He does, He invites us to take up a different form of protection. These new protective behaviours give space for our vulnerable places to become more deeply known and strengthened. These new ways focus on caring for, attending to and nurturing the wounded heart, whereas our old protective ways denied it.

These new protective ways can take on many forms, however their function is always the same—listen to and honor the heart, acknowledge its vulnerabilities and offer self-compassion and validation throughout the process.

Physical Healing—An Example of Old and New Protection

As a nurse, I appreciate the importance of protection from the beginning to the end of the healing process in our physical bodies. Imagine you are mountain biking with friends, you fall, cut yourself badly and suspect you have broken your leg. First aid is paramount! Your friends compress the bleeding and create a make-shift splint for your leg. Although the bleeding has stopped and the limb immobilized—these measures are temporary. In order for your wounds to heal well and for there to be no long-term limitations, you need to get to a professional who can provide you the necessary care.

At the hospital, in order for the doctor to help, she needs to examine your wounds. The compresses and the make-shift splint have to be removed. Although these measures were appropriate and helpful earlier, now they create an obstacle to receiving care. The process of removing the old protections can feel painful and unsettling.

Once the doctor determines the necessary tests and care, your wound is covered again with bandages and a cast applied. The old bandages and splint are not appropriate for this new care. Their job is done. The bone needs a more secure form of immobilization, the laceration stitches, and sterile bandages cover the wound to keep it clean and dry. All these measures promote and protect healing of the wound.

In time, the fracture heals, the cast is removed, and the stitches dissolve—but more care is still required to optimize healing. At this stage, physiotherapy begins. The goal of physiotherapy is to strengthen the muscles and ligaments that have weakened in the process—both from the injury and the immobilization. This protective step takes time and cannot be skipped, minimized or accelerated. In this stage of care, you listen to your body, rest when you need to, attend physiotherapy, and eat a balanced diet. Although the cast is off and you feel less restricted, it is unwise to resume mountain biking, lift heavy weights, or try new sports. To protect and promote healing, boundaries exist. The wound is still vulnerable.

Protecting Our Hearts

As we promote health in our places of emotional pain, we too need to protect them. Although the protection we need is unique to our areas of wounding and vulnerabilities, I have come to realize there are common themes.

Know Your Vulnerabilities

As we move forward in our journeys, there are two key areas of vulnerability: First, we need to be aware of the unpleasant emotions we struggle to release and second, we need to be aware of the behaviors we turn to, to avoid or soothe our pain.

Unpleasant emotions

Emotions are not good or bad. However, some are more unpleasant to experience than others. As we attend to our wounded hearts, we become aware of the unpleasant emotions we have avoided or soothed. Feelings like shame, fear, guilt, self-contempt, and insecurity arise. As we invite Jesus into these places of pain, He frees us from their grip on our lives. This freedom is a process. As we walk out our freedom, particular events induce these unpleasant emotions and can trigger us back into hiding and avoidance.

Old, Familiar Patterns of Protection

Our old ways of protection worked temporally. Because we have already partnered with specific behaviors or are familiar with them generationally—we are vulnerable to choosing them when we are triggered. We may also find that we're ingenious at creating new ways to avoid pain.

Practice Self Compassion and Curiosity

Self-compassion and curiosity are great (and healthy) protectors! They help and encourage us in our vulnerable places because they are abundant in grace! Jesus extends abundant grace to us in our need and we can ask Him to help us take this stance toward our own hearts.

As we approach our wounded hearts with kindness, we can be curious about our emotional responses. For many of us, this needs to be an intentional process as the more familiar voices of shame, criticism, and judgement speak loudly.

As we extend self-compassion and curiosity, we engage with our hearts rather than turn away from them. We begin to grow in self-confidence as we appreciate our own sources of resilience and courage. And, when we fail, we embrace our humanity. Extending grace dismantles shame and perfectionism and encourages self-respect.

Adopting a stance of curiosity enables one to discover more. The intention is to wonder, to expand our understanding, and to appreciate more—rather than judge, berate and belittle ourselves.

In this stance of curiosity, our thoughts are realigned. We challenge false belief structures that have told us things like we are lazy, stupid, a failure or alone. Extending curiosity we ask, why would I think that? Is that true? Why did that come to mind? When did I first feel that?

As Jesus wooed me with His love and friendship, He empowered me to lay down my defences of silence and emotion stuffing and give Him access to my wounded heart. His presence and compassion spoke loudly in my places of emptiness and shame.

To move forward, I continue to need to listen to my heart, to practice self-compassion and curiosity. During vulnerable times, I draw on the grace Jesus has for me and offer it to myself. Perfection is not possible, because I am human. Through self-compassion, I understand my old choices and the rationale for choosing them. I have learned, and continue to learn, that I cannot integrate parts of me with which I am in conflict. I often challenge my own thinking, and ask questions to deepen my self-awareness rather than deny or partner with words of shame. Many of my vulnerable areas are strengthening and for that I give God the glory.

Self-compassion and curiosity offer grace, build self-love, and honor our humanity. As our vulnerable places become stronger, our safeguards lessen and, at times, change. Nevertheless, as we *are being* sanctified, we will always need protection.

Chapter 18

Hardship Leads to the Embrace of Paradox
by David Gotts

David Gotts, Founder of International China Concern, has been connected to Journey Canada since 1999. He lives in Vancouver with his wife, Linda and son, Jamie.

What is strength? My answer to this question has changed over the years. How I would have answered as a teenager versus how I would answer now is definitely very different.

For me to answer the question, "What is strength?" with anything other than a dictionary definition requires me to look back across my life, at the many circumstances that have, at times, been painful and yet have led me to gradually become a stronger person.

As with every story, fact or fiction, you have to have a beginning. For me, that beginning happened in May of 1987. I was sixteen when I responded to Jesus' invitation to follow Him. The experience of coming to understand what Jesus had done for me, combined with His offer of a new life filled me with such gratitude. There was a delight in giving Him my life and yet sometimes I wonder whether that decision to surrender ALL ought to have been a more sobering one, particularly if I knew the perseverance and sacrifice the journey ahead would require of me. Still, the nature of coming to know Jesus was a joyful one and I gratefully launched myself into this new life He offered.

From that point a journey into perseverance and sacrifice began, and with it and through it came a strength of which I could have never conceived.

Within a year, there came a gradual revelation that God was calling me to leave my family, friends, job, and basically all I knew and move to the other side of the world. The growing conviction of what was being asked of me felt gentle but clear. Saying "yes" to that call was both exciting and challenging. There was a definite cost to it. I soon discovered how big a cost it was when I landed in Hong Kong in September of 1990 to begin a new kind of life serving God in missions. I didn't know it at the time, but saying "yes" to that opportunity was also a saying "goodbye" to all that I knew and was familiar with.

The first months of that time were extremely tough. I was terribly homesick and desperately wanted to get back on a plane and return home. But I couldn't, as I knew that Jesus had asked this of me. Whilst feeling the loss of what I had given up with each passing day, I was also coming to understand what being called to sacrifice for the sake of Christ and "giving my life to Him" truly meant.

Standing in a Chinese state-run orphanage in January of 1993, facing the reality of the situation of abandoned children with disabilities was overwhelming. The only way to cope was to numb my feelings. Witnessing death and suffering on a scale of that magnitude caused everything within me to want to run the other way. To say that Jesus' invitation to actively step towards that situation was not easy would be understating the reality of how I felt. The invitation by Jesus to immerse my life in it and to begin the work of International China Concern was a seemingly impossible ask. I actually did a pretty good impression of Jonah, running in the opposite direction for nine months. The primary feeling was one of wanting this "cup" to pass from me. The cup did not pass. Instead, because of God's desire to transform both the world and each one of us for His glory, the invitation from Jesus persisted. I came to discover that His love for China's children with disabilities was unrelenting, as was His desire for me to walk in His plans and His ways. I think I grew a little stronger on that day in October 1993, when I came to realise that my fear of inadequate strength was not a good enough reason to run away. Instead, I was being called to trust that I would be doing this work not on my own strength but by the indwelling of His unfathomable strength. It was His amazing grace that enabled me to say "yes."

As you can imagine, starting a Christian, compassion-based ministry in Communist China, heralded numerous opportunities to develop strength, experience sacrifice, and grow in perseverance. Working in China was challenging, particularly when working with the Chinese government. As I look back at those years, I felt a little like Joshua and Caleb; I knew that taking "the promised land" was going to involve many battles. I had no idea, when I embarked on this journey almost 30 years ago, how hard it would be. Yet I wouldn't change a thing, because the hardship of the journey has been an integral part of Jesus being formed in me.

In the summer of 1999, I took a three-month sabbatical from China and went to Canada. I had gone because of a growing sense of inner turmoil that was leading down the road to crisis. Stepping into a season of counselling, and taking part in the Journey Canada training was not easy for a young, British guy that had no language to describe his internal life and struggles. I have often described that time as being like open heart surgery. It was momentous, but also scary and painful. I didn't know who I would be when I came out the other side, but I did know that my internal pain had led me to the place where I felt like giving up on following Jesus. Beginning to know myself through that process of opening, acknowledging, and cleansing was painful end yet freeing. I saw, for the first time, my own brokenness and came to know how weak I truly was. Pressing in each day during that summer wasn't easy, but by the end of it I knew it had been so worth it, as I rediscovered my faith in deeper and more meaningful ways.

I don't quite know when I fully realized this scriptural truth that when we are weak, then we are strong[25] (because of His strength), but I think I can trace the roots of it back to what began in that transformational summer in Canada in 1999. I know you may not want to hear this, but, for me at least, the knowledge of my weakness has continued to grow more profound since that time. It grew as I walked through my fears and insecurities as I dated the woman that I would marry. God placed before me a woman who was beautiful in the truest sense of the word—both inside and out. I was unprepared for how weak I would feel as I battled those fears and insecurities. I am so thankful for the friends that loved me and prayed for me, who stood with me as I pressed on until, amazingly, in December of 2001 I finally arrived at a place of feeling certain, sure, confident: ready to propose and marry this amazing woman God had led me to.

However, as with any good story, I saved the most dramatic for last.

My second son, Kieran, was born in 2008. Our family was complete. In addition to Jamie, our then two-year-old, we now had this strawberry blond, blue-eyed baby with a slightly wonky and endearing smile.

You can imagine the shock when we found ourselves rushing Kieran to the ER late one night. The next few days that followed are still something of a hazy, sleep-deprived blur. What is not hazy is the moment when we learned the news that Kieran had been born with a neurological condition that would affect him for the rest of his life. Learning about his condition and dealing with the unpredictability of his daily seizures was exhausting.

---

[25] 2 Cor. 12:10

As we learned to help Kieran and give him a life with some semblance of normality, we were hit by the diagnosis of cancer near his brainstem at the age of three. The diagnosis left us feeling devastated, utterly helpless and weak, as did the ten-month long journey of treatment. Cancer compounded Kieran's disabilities, requiring ongoing intensive care and therapy in order to foster his development. The recurrence of his cancer, along with a terminal diagnosis at the age of 8 broke our hearts, as did those last weeks in Canuck Place Children's Hospice as we said goodbye to him.

Whilst it may be almost impossible to believe, that period of time was both painful and heartbreaking, as well as beautiful and sacred. In the midst of the sadness, it felt like we saw life in technicolor—every moment was precious. Caring for Kieran in the midst of the sadness and exhaustion was so challenging, but even in the darkest times, as we pressed on, we felt that God was fulfilling His promise from Isaiah 45:3 to give us "treasures in the darkness."

Here's what I learned from those amazing eight and a half years we had with Kieran. Each of those hard times, each of those moments was like an invitation. It was an invitation to both sacrifice and persevere. Many times, we had to sacrifice our expectations of what we wanted Kieran's life to be, as well as persevering in both trusting God's plans and caring for our amazing son. Sacrifice and perseverance were the gateway to strength as we said "yes" to those invitations.

So, if you now ask me the question, "What is strength?" here is what I will tell you...

Strength is saying "yes" to the many invitations from Jesus to trust Him, while feeling inadequate for the tasks. Strength is, paradoxically, coming to understand your own weakness and yet choosing to obey and follow where He leads. Some of those invitations will fill you with joy, some will require sacrifice, many will require perseverance, but no matter what kind of invitation is given, stepping towards those invitations will grow your dependence on Jesus and, in the process, make you stronger than you ever thought possible.

For when I am weak, then I am strong.

-2 Corinthians 12:10

Chapter 19

Courage
Facing Reality—With Jesus
by Claude Provost

Claude Provost is an entrepreneur and artist living in Montreal. He has been involved with leading and growing Journey programs in Quebec since 1994.

Reflecting back on some childhood memories, I can remember the age when the training wheels came off and I tasted the freedom that a "real" bicycle could offer. It required the help and support of a running dad holding the seat so I wouldn't crash at the first sensation of being on my own. The taste of freedom was greater than the risk of hurting myself. To move forward on my own, I needed to find the courage to face the fear of the unknown, to confront the insecurities of falling, and accept the risk of being laughed at. At the time, what I didn't know was that I had to make a choice. I had to find the courage to trust someone else and believe I could surmount the crowd of fears in my heart that would allow me to stand on my own.

Courage, in its simplest definition, encompasses not only making a choice, but the ability to look at adversity straight on. As we move forward in the midst of difficulties, we need to face our fears and insecurities. Courage is the strength that inhabits our soul while facing danger or suffering and allows us to persevere.
The choice that we have made to follow Jesus is certainly one that carries intensity and fear of the unknown. It involves abdicating our own free will to accept the path He has chosen for us. This path normally includes facing the reality of our past life and the

brokenness it carries. It means facing some challenges or life-changing choices which can often be counter cultural. Basically, the journey we embarked on is one that requires courage and resilience—the ability to bounce back after a difficult experience.

Like a child who needs training wheels to reach the confidence to grow and be able to ride on a "real" bicycle, I needed the Father to stand by me and nurture me to grow and be equipped to face life's challenges. My initial experience of God's love was a revelation that carried the assurance of not being alone, the strength to move forward, and the ability, without hesitation, to go back to Him in times of hardships. Most of all, I felt empowered with the courage to stand for my spiritual convictions.

To be able to ride a bicycle, one needs to develop balance. Spiritually, I feel one can find balance in life by fostering a loving relationship with Jesus. The Holy Spirit offers this balance. He is the initiator of the relationship and the one who sustains it. The ability to grow in confidence requires a constant priority for his presence in our life that will, over time, offer us the sustaining courage to face what's ahead. The assurance of His love is the basis for my courage.

Over time, I felt my journey into wholeness became blurred by the broken areas from my past that overshadowed my heart. Doubt clouded my understanding of the Father's love. Wounded and fearful, I felt stuck to the point that I couldn't move forward, feeling like quicksand was pulling me down. Even during these difficult times, when I was in doubt, I found the courage to stand because I had experienced the Father's faithfulness in the past.

Throughout my journey, God has led me many times to stand at the edge of a cliff, facing the void of emptiness before me while asking me to take the next step in making a life-changing decision filled with unknowns. Repeatedly, He has provided for me a way to move forward into freedom. I recall one such time of prayer; in the Father's presence, He asked me to release to Him what I thought was my identity. Standing before Him, feeling rather vulnerable, defenseless and exposed, not knowing what would happen or where my security would come from, I had to refer back to times when He had shown me mercy so that my response would be to accept His will over mine. As a result, He has reclaimed my true identity.

Does that mean that courage is the first element that I draw from when I have to face adversity? Of course not! The journey we are on is filled with life's experiences that differ and are personal to each of us. They are often influenced by the way we feel about them or by the counsel or opinions of others in regard to them.

We may know, in our hearts, what the right course to choose is, but sometimes we find that the voice of our fears and insecurities, or peer pressure—is much louder than the still small voice of truth in our hearts. Which voice do you truly desire to follow? Can you ask for grace to have the courage to follow your deepest convictions in the choices that lie before you?

Our emotional state is unreliable when it comes to making a choice. As we are called to model our lives and values on Jesus, a renewed commitment to His love becomes a precise and dependable foundation.

The Father has implemented guidelines to safeguard us, and by keeping these instructions we are able to find the courage to live life and face adversities. The freedom that we feel while riding a bicycle is the outcome of exercises, practice, trials and errors, which gives the child a sense of assurance. So it is for us. To find courage, we need to practice the presence of the Holy Spirit, exercise and develop our friendship with Jesus, and evolve in our ability to rely upon our Father in our trials and errors.

As we read 2 Peter 1, we find guidance: "His divine power has given us everything required for life and godliness through the knowledge of him who called us by his own glory and goodness. ...For this very reason, make every effort to supplement your faith with goodness...

knowledge… self-control… endurance (courage)… godliness… affection, and love."[26]

Our response to this call will last a lifetime and is subject to daily renewal.

Perhaps as we read these verses, we are being challenged by a number of questions as there will be times throughout our journey when the right choices will become harder to make. When we are tired, bored, lonely, we don't feel like moving forward, or we don't feel like healing is happening fast enough. We don't feel God's presence or we may even be struggling with the desire to find something more pleasurable while facing a struggle. In these situations, we are faced with a dilemma.

Pain has the propensity to bring our focus back to ourselves. At times when we might feel like we can't move on, a trusted friend can also provide courage. God has given us a community for support. None of us can be freed through our own efforts. We need God and we need each other. In a way, God is asking us to encourage and support one another towards the liberation we all long for. Journey has made provision for a safe place to build profound friendships; men and women I can trust with my inmost secrets and despairs. Their counsel has often led me back to the Light.

Jesus has demonstrated to us that transformation has taken place in the tomb. His dead body was enlivened with a new and life-giving energy. This is also a promise that transformation can happen in our own experience of darkness, disappointment, or the death of our dreams, but it requires the courage to change our way of seeing things. It's about finding that source of truth in the core of our being.

This capacity for change can become a constant reality enabling us to live our lives to the fullest and grow from the trauma of the past.

---

[26] 2 Pet.1:3-7

We consciously have to decide to bring any places of emptiness in our own life into the light of the Holy Spirit.

As our lives move on, we may be tempted to race ahead in our healing journey and seek answers connected to some broken areas in our life which have not yet resurfaced. In these moments we need the balance of the Holy Spirit. Only He knows the right pace and our capacity to endure, as well as the timing to be able to face whatever broken area is requiring His attention. It is He who calls us, empowers us to make the journey into darkness and instills life into our woundedness. He knows more than we do, just like the father holding the child's bicycle knows when to release him.

As we travel on, we need to empty our hands from everything that is keeping us from receiving all the graces Jesus has died for and still longs to give us.

We can choose to slip back into our old ways, or we can choose with courage to let Love transform the way we live.

Chapter 20

We Never Grow Beyond Need
by Daniel Komori

Daniel Komori is the associate executive director of Journey Canada. He enjoys brewing beer and home DIY projects. He lives in Calgary, Alberta with his family.

One of the core lessons taught at Journey is that the journey of healing is a process. The ongoing reality of lifelong dependence on God will not change, no matter the dramatic encounters we've had with Jesus, or the deep levels of cleansing and renewal we've experienced in our hearts. The call to be open to God's intimate touch and life-giving Spirit remains a daily path to be walked and embraced. We never grow beyond a desperate need for God's presence in our lives. Learning to accept and live out the truth that healing is a journey is, for many, a journey all its own.

I first came to the Journey Discipleship Course with the expectation that I was committing to a *very long course* (back then it was 30 weeks!) to finally put to rest some of the lifelong struggles I'd been facing around sin, weakness, and addiction. Taking Journey was a commitment I was willing to make to deal with my inner struggles "once and for all." I was going to pursue God and place the last "nail in the coffin" in regards to overcoming the most stubborn areas of brokenness in my life.

As with anyone who seeks to engage in the Journey course honestly, I found myself struggling as I faced the challenge of being vulnerable in small groups—confessing what was going on in my heart and facing many areas of past pain and shame. However, I was rewarded and indeed blessed to have marvelous encounters with Jesus where I was able to receive life-giving truth, heartwarming God-embraces, and strengthening words of His affirmation and care towards me. But how did all those experiences affect my overall sense of feeling whole?

With the mentality with which I came to the course, I thought those wonderful experiences should strengthen me and lead to a place where my struggles and weaknesses would go away, since they had now been "dealt with." Shouldn't my deep and genuine encounters with God free me from struggling with bouts of anxiety and insecurity? Shouldn't those moments where I saw Jesus with great clarity, and feeling His love so tangibly lead me to never denying Him again?

I had to learn the lesson that healing is a journey, and a long one. No single experience was going to fully "fix" my heart, and my longing and need for God would remain. In fact, my ache for God would actually increase as time went on.

Two prominent New Testament figures helped me embrace the reality that God would indeed not take away all my struggles, or my ongoing experience of need. Paul and Peter helped me to see that my experience was not an aberration, but was in fact the way of growth God envisions for all His people.

The apostle Paul famously relates in 2 Corinthians how he asked God on multiple occasions to remove a "thorn in the flesh" from his life.[27] Nobody knows what this thorn was, but it was clearly some type of ongoing difficult experience which Paul would have rather not have had in his life. If anyone deserved a unique touch of God in their lives, it was Paul, who was truly one-of-a-kind in

---

[27] 2 Cor. 12:7-8

terms of his commitment and suffering for the faith. Yet God's surprising response to this great and hard-working apostle was to say He would not remove this difficulty, as the very place of his felt experience of weakness was to be the conduit through which Paul would experience the ongoing grace of God. For Paul, ongoing intimacy and growth with God did not translate to being rid of some of the most stubborn areas of weakness in his life. God's mysterious ways of imparting grace required that his need remain.

The apostle Peter learned a similar lesson. Peter is well-known as someone who had wild swings in his understanding and expression of faith. He would be the first in line to step out in faith, jumping off the boat into the sea towards Jesus, and he also showed keen insight regarding the unique identity of Jesus when nobody else saw clearly who He was. Yet there were times Peter completely misunderstood the mission of Jesus and his ultimate denial of Jesus led to him hiding away in shame and fear. To Peter, a man who fluctuated between an unmovable faith one day and a fearful heart the next, Jesus' instruction also offers us the insight that a maturing of faith involves a growing, not lessening, dependence on the mercy and grace of God.

> Very truly I tell you, when you were younger you dressed yourself and went where you wanted; but when you are old you will stretch out your hands, and someone else will dress you and lead you where you do not want to go.

-John 21:18

In the last recorded conversation we have between them, Jesus tells Peter that his path of growth and development would entail a wider embrace of the unknown and a greater need to trust that provision would come outside of his own doing and making. Much like Paul, the picture of "spiritual maturity" given to Peter is not one of arriving at a state of having less need, or experiencing less struggle, but is a picture of *increase* in felt need, and a growth in trust toward the ongoing outpouring of the grace of God.

Healing is a journey which has been hard for me to embrace. However, these lessons given to Peter and Paul help shape and reform my own narrow vision, a vision which tends to perceive spiritual progression as marked by feelings of internal completion—never again wrestling with bouts of temptation or insecurity. The witness of Scripture and Jesus' ways of dealing with His beloved followers paints the picture that healing is indeed a lifelong journey and is actually a mark of His ongoing work in our lives. I will never grow beyond my need for God as it is the means by which He continues His mighty work in me. Hallelujah.

Chapter 21

Acceptance
Longing for Belonging
by Mark Elvin

*M*ark Elvin is a spiritual director, painter and former skateboarder. He has coordinated the Edmonton program for more than 25 years.

First day at a new school in rural Alberta, halfway through grade six. I walk in and know nobody. It felt odd: I did not know where to sit. I did not know where I belonged. Lost would be a good descriptor. I soon found out that making friends was not going to be easy—the city school I had previously attended was in my neighborhood and most of my friends went there. My sense of acceptance had been somewhat fragile before the change and was now pronounced. I did not fit the culture, I did not get the jokes, my clothes stood out, I was encouraged to fight. Soon I was pegged as an outsider who did not, could not, belong. Many ignored me like I was not there, but a few took a fancy to making my life miserable.

I tried just being me, but everything I did I was picked on for—a wrong look or comment or just because I was there. Eventually I wanted to disappear and not be seen. The few connections I did have shared the same place at the bottom of the social pile. Eventually I learned how to blend in, almost to the point of disappearing. Avoiding unwanted attention was a good day. The cost for this was high: no meaningful relationships, not being able to be me. The longing to connect, to feel like I belonged, to feel included and welcomed was painful. I did not know how to act without risking ridicule. School became a place to survive. Who I was was not known, not even by me.

Our journey for acceptance starts in the family. Acceptance is not innate, it is built in us. We discover that we are welcomed, have space at the table and, no matter what, we are loved. Through acceptance, our uniqueness is discovered and encouraged. Lack of acceptance leaves a vulnerability, and the more vulnerable, the greater challenge it is to feel acceptance.

Most of us struggle to some degree with acceptance. Where do I sit? At the back and hide or at the front so that everyone can look at me? *Are* they looking at me? Am I wearing the right clothes? Is my hair the right length, style? Will I be accepted, rejected, ignored, or worse? So uncertain about any of the choices. What if I make the wrong one? The feelings can be overwhelming. The uncertainty can feel paralyzing.

For me, the enemy of acceptance was failure. Failure can be a wrong choice, a bad choice, something that garners unwanted attention. Failure puts acceptance at risk. Even now while writing this, I wrestle with these questions: Am I achieving what is expected of me? Will this be good enough to publish? Will I experience disappointment?

There are many scriptures that speak about God's acceptance. Two that continue to be important for me are Romans 8:38-39 and Psalm 139. These stand out because it's hard to believe that they're true. The language of intimacy in Psalm 139, of God's knowledge of me, is uncomfortable (except verses 23 and 24) because I anticipate that there is bad to be exposed. But the Psalm insists that God knows me *and* loves me. The same is true for Romans 8—not being able to go anywhere to escape God's love does not feel possible. Personal acceptance of me *as me,* right here and now, has always been difficult. If I cannot accept myself, no one can—not even God.

To my mind, being good, doing good, or at least looking good is acceptance. But that is not what these scriptures are saying.

God has used three points of reference to challenge my view of acceptance. First was what I call a day-vision, not a dream. I was at work in my office some 30 years ago. I was wrestling with my life. Married, two kids, a Christian for eight years. I also had hidden sin, sexual sin. No matter how hard I tried to stop I could not. If anyone knew, including my wife, I would lose everything. I so desperately wanted to be a good Christian husband and father. On this day, I had turned off the lights in my office and prayed a desperate prayer: "God if you are real, I want to be real no matter what."

Immediately a scene opened before me, a gray scene. I was in a small boat without oars. Everything was gray—the sky, water, boat, and me. I thought, this is how I feel, no real life, everything is fake. Then I saw Jesus sitting on a rock on the shore, the boat stopped at the shore and Jesus motioned me to come to him. I went with my hands in my pocket expecting Jesus to inform me of all that I had done wrong, everything that was not acceptable. When I got near enough, Jesus grabbed me, pulled me into His lap and said, "Mark, I love you." No condemnation, no lecture on how to be better, no "this is your last chance." Full acceptance even when I thought my life was a shamble. My carefully-constructed outer shell did not hide me from Jesus. He knew and loved me, accepted me.

The second point of reference was when I was getting ready to attend the first Journey Intensive retreat week in 1995. Journey had given me language to understand God's acceptance and love and that this was the starting point in finding life, having hope. I was able to share with two couples in our home group what I had been learning, but kept some particulars out of the discussion since the details would likely cause me to not be accepted. As it turned out, I had to write a short testimony for the application process. In the testimony, I was quite clear about my struggles and the process that I was in. I felt that the Lord wanted me to share this with these couples. I was scared, but I did it. I imagined that they would likely keep a kind but respectable distance from me. What I experienced instead was an immediate warm embrace and gratitude for sharing.

The third point of reference God used to challenge my view of acceptance is the ongoing journey of community and accountability. As I said earlier, I believed that failure was the enemy of acceptance. I love accountability, especially when I have nothing to confess or report a weakness. Failure is so hard to admit, yet it has been through sharing my failures, wrestling with my weaknesses, that I find acceptance. I learn again and again that who I am does not need to be something acceptable, but just to be me, real and vulnerable. I am not yet at the place where St. Paul declares in 2 Corinthians 12: "But he said to me, 'My grace is sufficient for you, for my power is perfected in weakness.' Therefore, I will most gladly boast all the more about my weaknesses, so that Christ's power may reside in me."[28]

I was so afraid to be real, to show the real me, warts and all. I thought acceptance was what others wanted. I thought acceptance was what I perceived to be acceptable. Yet acceptance starts with me just as I am, through Jesus. I cannot accept myself without Him. This includes being accepted when I fail.
Failure is not the cost of acceptance, but through failure we learn acceptance.

---

[28] 2 Cor. 12:9

Chapter 22

Delight
Pleasure is not the Enemy
by Janet Wright-Smit

Janet Wright-Smit is an Ontario photographer and bon vivant. *She is a long-time coordinator in Journey's discipleship course. She considers serving in Journey a true vocation.*

> "Passion; vibrancy; tremendously enjoyable;
> anticipation; excitement; deep, quiet pleasure;
> a holiness; things that melt my heart."

If asked for my spontaneous understanding of delight, these adjectives come immediately to mind as the Janet of today. I wish I could write this in all the colours that might be a visual representation of delight. Imagine it... Can you see them?

When you hear the word "delight," what comes to mind? How have you experienced delight, what are your thoughts, beliefs, memories? Has it been positive to experience delight? Has delight been thick with secrecy and sin? Has it been literally "pure delight"? Can you share memorable moments of delight, or have many been fake, false, smoke and mirrors, and allowing brief pleasure but long pain? Most of us have tasted delight in all of the above, haven't we?

Let's look at both dictionary and biblical definitions of this wonderful word. Merriam Webster defines delight this way:

verb: to take great pleasure; to give keen enjoyment. E.g., "delighted in playing the guitar."

noun: a high degree of gratification or pleasure; extreme satisfaction; something that gives great pleasure.

synonyms: exuberate, exult, pleasure, joy, treat, glory, jubilate, rejoice.[29]

My Bible dictionary tells me that delight or something similar is mentioned about 110 times in Scripture. It says, "Two of the most common Hebrew terms for delight are *hepes*, 'to bend towards, to be inclined towards [an object or person], 'and *rasa*, 'to delight or take pleasure in.'"[30]

Many of us, if raised in a church environment, have grown up in what I call a "both world."

We have the both-ness of the influence of legalism and religiosity, which often have strong elements of rules and guidelines for "right living." If our parents adhered to these, we as children and youth would have innocently absorbed the same indoctrination. The rules would have been our truth and our grid against which to measure right from wrong. If we lived and socialized within this bubble it would be years, if ever, before we examined and challenged our "normal."

It may sound extreme to read, yet one does not need to experience being raised in a cult to have these experiences. In Journey, we hear

---

[29] *Merriam-Webster*, https://www.merriam-webster.com/dictionary/delight

[30] Daniel Aiken, "Delight," in *Baker's Evangelical Dictionary of Biblical Theology* (1996). https://www.biblestudytools.com/dictionaries/bakers-evangelical-dictionary/delight.html

many testimonies from people in rather mainstream traditional churches, who until Journey, were heavy with the weight of shame, guilt, self-hatred, for things they had chosen to experience and the consequences from them.

Conversely, we have exposure to "the world, the flesh and the devil," each of which are the antagonists to our secure familiar world—they poke and tempt and woo us with a cacophony of, "You deserve this," "Everyone does this, it's normal," "Just this once," or "You're not hurting anyone, no one knows." Interestingly, our areas of temptation are tailor-made specifically for us alone. What might trap me in its web might bore you or be irrelevant and vice versa. The majority of our world culture markets delight in the context of self-indulgence, of few limitations, of being one's own god, and it is offered in nearly irresistible ways.

Anyone feeling the delight thus far? If you actually are, show me where! I'm kidding... But stay with me—here comes the hope factor, the possibilities, the WAY better way, the "Jesus, you are awesome" way!

From my teenage years, I was an artistic creative streamed into math and science academics. I longed to study art at university but my father, who was a professor, discouraged this firmly, as in, "No." So instead, I entered nursing and remained in that profession until I didn't, many years later. I felt like a beige person in beige clothes against a beige wall, screaming and begging to be noticed and hoping to not be seen.

I entered Journey as a frozen, disconnected, multi-mask-wearing shy woman, with little self-awareness and no identity except who I'd been told I was, verbally and non-verbally. I was a stellar actress and literally no-one in my world knew the Janet inside. They saw confidence and colour and leadership and so much more. Some previous therapy had started me on a healing path and it launched me into the Journey program.

Experientially, the most astounding things began to unfold—literal DELIGHT in all the ways!

I learned who Jesus said I was, He clarified my identity in Him, He called out the unique ways of being which He'd wired into my DNA. He instilled a comfortable confidence in being me, unapologetically so. He soothed the trauma and bruises where the lack of a father, and much misogyny, had paralyzed me. During times of prayer, I literally felt grave clothes unwrap from my neck and a voice: "Rise up within me and come forth!"

In my past, what I might have called delight would be mostly excessive self-pleasure experiences like overeating ("I deserve this"), over shopping ("retail therapy works!"), over-busyness ("this is admirable and brings lots of compliments"). I even then loved to give and serve and received delight in so doing.

In my present, experiences of pure delight would be examples of drinking in the beauty of a garden centre in spring; standing in the library to choose delightful reads; soaking in worship and song, lost in adoration of my Triune God; beholding the birth of a baby in all the miraculous-ness of it; dipping my brush into wet paint and bringing it to the canvas; the delight of preparing food; table scaping; classical music; and slowly sipping a glass of Pinot Noir whilst waiting for loved ones to arrive—an extra meaningful moment is to see fathers with their little girls, clearly cherishing them. Scripture has much, much to say about delight and I know, totally, that as we grow in intimacy with our Triune God, as we experience His delight in us and ours in Him, we move into that marvelous place of fullness and freedom He planned for us all along.

The once beige, on beige, on beige Janet now lives fully and vibrantly in delight. In a delight-FULL world of colour, passion, art—creativity in all aspects of life, delighting in things beyond my wildest dreams (mentoring teens, photographing a fashion shoot every week, speaking at events, painting, growing an online following with photography and emotional support… and more). I sense the joy of my First Love as He observes His girl uncontainably living His perfect life for her, contagiously sharing with all who dare to come into her path.

SELAH

Section 4—Traveling Companions

So far, we have used the journey metaphor to talk about various phases of pursuing the spiritual life. In these final two sections we'll turn our attention to some other aspects of what it means to travel. One of the great things about this road is that God does not expect us to travel it alone and, in fact, through scripture it is clear that we *cannot* travel alone. We need help.

The people who accompany us take various forms. Perhaps most obviously, we are asked to travel in community with the people of God as part of a local church, but we are also accompanied by others—family, friends, saints, those who have written about their own journeys and left behind a record of what they have learned. It is one of the great and wonderful truths that we are accompanied on this journey by real people—people who we know and are alive with us now, and people who lived in the past.

The ultimate guide and companion for the journey is the Holy Spirit, Who illuminates and reveals the path for us and Who explains the map to us—helping us to comprehend scripture—and Who speaks to us as we seek to navigate the world around us. This section begins with a few different people thinking about the significance of the Holy Spirit in their lives.

-GL

"Revelation Road: The Road to Emmaus" by
Toni Dolfo-Smith - Acrylic on Canvas

For Friends Only

(for John and Teckla Clark)

Ours yet not ours, being set apart
As a shrine to friendship,
Empty and silent most of the year,
This room awaits from you
What you alone, as visitor, can bring,
A weekend of personal life.

In a house backed by orderly woods,
Facing a tractored sugar-beet country,
Your working hosts engaged to their stint,
You are unlike to encounter
Dragons or romance: were drama a craving,
You would not have come.

Books we do have for almost any
Literate mood, and notepaper, envelopes,
For a writing one (to "borrow" stamps
Is the mark of ill-breeding):
Between lunch and tea, perhaps a drive;
After dinner, music or gossip.

Should you have troubles (pets will die
Lovers are always behaving badly)
And confession helps, we will hear it,
Examine and give our counsel:
If to mention them hurts too much,
We shall not be nosey.

Easy at first, the language of friendship

Is, as we soon discover,
Very difficult to speak well, a tongue

With no cognates, no resemblance
To the galimatias of nursery and bedroom,
Court rhyme or shepherd's prose,

And, unless spoken often, soon goes rusty.
Distance and duties divide us,
But absence will not seem an evil
If it make our re-meeting
A real occasion. Come when you can:
Your room will be ready.

In Tum-Tum's reign a tin of biscuits
On the bedside table provided
For nocturnal munching. Now weapons have changed,
And the fashion of appetites:
There, for sunbathers who count their calories,
A bottle of mineral water.

Felicissima notte! May you fall at once
Into a cordial dream, assured
That whoever slept in this bed before
Was also someone we like,
That within the circle of our affection
Also you have no double.

                                        -W.H. Auden

Chapter 23

The Holy Spirit
Our Counselor and Friend
Various Authors

Getting a good, healthy perspective on God is a challenge for all of us. We bring all kinds of baggage and mistaken assumptions into our relationship with Him. Nowhere is this more apparent than in our relationship with the Holy Spirit. The Spirit can feel poorly defined, scary, and something less than a full person who is part of the triune God. Scholar Gordon Fee has amended the creedal confession of the Trinity to reflect the way many of us feel:

> We believe in God the Father, Almighty, Maker of heaven and earth; and we believe in Jesus Christ his Son; but we are not so sure about the Holy Spirit.[31]

For this chapter, we asked several leaders within Journey to provide us with one word that describes their experience of the Holy Spirit—to wrestle with both the ambiguity and the joy that surrounds Him. We also asked them for a brief explanation about why they chose that particular word.

---

[31] Gordon D. Fee, *Paul, the Spirit, and the People of God* (2011).

Toni Dolfo-Smith—Ambivalence
AMBIVALENCE... The good boy in me immediately wanted another word, something more sacred, powerful, spiritual. But AMBIVALENCE is the one that stuck!

A fundamentalist upbringing where we spoke of the "Holy Ghost" rather than the "Holy Spirit," left my developing imagination confusing disembodied, floating beings and eerie campfire stories, with the person and workings of the Holy Spirit. That is where I believe my AMBIVALENCE began.

A late teenage encounter with God convinced me that the Holy Spirit was both real, and always with me even when I was not aware of His presence in my sensory being. From that time on, it has often seemed that being in relationship with the Holy Spirit has meant difficult choices and life-altering decisions. My most memorable conversations with Him have been about giving up things I prize, and losing things I love in order to receive what He is offering me.

Though I once experienced His whispers as commands, I now see them as loving invitations to embrace more of the life Jesus died to give me. AMBIVALENCE may often still be my initial response to Him, but the longer I have listened to His counsel, the more readily I embrace what He asks of me.

Amy Donaldson—Convictor
Convictor and Convincer... These words were planted in my heart at the church I grew up in, which taught that we could be holy, even perfect, in this earthly life. The religious expectations spoke to me of the seriousness of my behaviour. I believed the Holy Ghost was my internal policeman, convicting me of my sinful ways and convincing me of His truth. My four years of Bible college deepened this belief, intensifying my shame and self-hatred as I never came close to measuring up. So, I "white-knuckled"

it—hiding behind duty and service, the bedrock of my relationship with God.

In my late twenties, I came to Journey, where I experienced compassion and grace especially around my behaviours. I began to see Jesus as a friend rather than a religious standard to meet. The Spirit of Christ became One who would whisper, "Amy, we are better than this." I would feel a nudge by the Spirit—in kindness—convicting and convincing me to discover and become more of who He created me to be. Convincing me of His Love, I now enjoy this Spirit-to-spirit union which enables me to thrive in generously-loving God, others, and myself.

Claude Provost—Transformer

My thoughts about the Holy Spirit are more encompassing than just a word, He is my All in All. And I am delighted by the notion that the Holy Spirit is the power that transforms my heart, my attitudes, my desires, my thought life, the choices that I make, my mistakes, and my downfalls. He has the ability to turn things around. If a day starts in the wrong direction, I can make the choice to stop and ask Him to transform my negative attitude and somehow, I eventually experience a shift. I'm connected with the One who empowers me to become fully alive to what is happening in my life. Even if some days the change is not imminent, I know I can depend on Him to bring about a transformation. He is infallible as the great transformer of mankind.

Mark Elvin —Unfamiliar

A word to describe the Holy Spirit—unfamiliar. I am aware that the Holy Spirit is there, but I tend to connect with either the Father or Jesus. I know in my head that the essence of the Father and the Son exists within me, yet I refer to that presence as Jesus. When I pray, it is almost always to the Father, with Jesus intermixed and on occasion I mention the Spirit. Sorting that out in distinction is difficult. I am aware when the Spirit moves me to pray in a particular way for someone or with someone. I receive pictures or words that appear to have meaning when ministering. When I personally experience the presence of Jesus, I don't consider that it may be the Holy Spirit. The Triune God is always together, I fully believe in the Spirit yet He remains cognitively unfamiliar.

Margot Shutt—Encourager

Along with her husband Ed, Margot Shutt is a long-time leader and program coordinator for Journey. She lives in Halifax.

Encourager... When I think of Holy Spirit, I think encouragement. When I don't think I can carry on, when I am at my lowest point or at my wits end, or that my strength is gone, somehow encouragement comes, often in ways I don't expect or hope for. It comes to lift me up, to move me beyond myself and my issues, to restore life.

At my lowest points, I've needed to hear those words of encouragement, the truths that I've lost or somehow can't find within myself or haven't understood. I've searched and attempted to connect beyond myself. I've reached out. It was Jesus I turned to—to find that special and personal connection, to find that deepening relationship I desired. And it was to Father God I turned as I sought the unwinding of many lies that I had believed about Him. Holy Spirit has seemingly been in the "back seat" to my desire for connection with Jesus and Father God. But was it the Holy Spirit that convicted me to do that in the first place? Have I given Holy Spirit enough credit for what's happened?

I know my times of deepest connection have most often come through spending time with Jesus. But, is it Jesus who gives me the beautiful picture my heart longs for? Or is it Holy Spirit who passes that along to me from Jesus? Who is it that settles my heart and convicts me of truths and direction? Was Holy Spirit the encourager who led to my looking up and out beyond myself in the first place? Message or medium? Or do those particular words even apply? You can't have one without the other, in my thinking. Maybe I can settle for a "divine mystery"—then I don't need to explain the what or how to myself!

I resonate with the word "interwoven," like fine linen. Strong and tenable. Three strands of love, of hope, of conviction working together to bring encouragement, to bring life. All are to be thanked, to be praised.

Does it really matter how it happens, as long as it does? I don't think so.

Rosemary Flaaten—Safe

I grew up in a church with charismatic practises rooted in dramatic conversion experiences. Outward displays of being "filled with the Spirit" were not only common but were often used as evidence of one's spiritual grandeur. I can recount numerous personal experiences where the sensational became distorted and misused. My encounters with the Holy Spirit, or more specifically, my encounters with people around me who were supposedly encountering the Spirit, was anything but safe.

CS Lewis allegorically declares that God is not safe, but He is good.[32] Jeremiah proclaims to the exiles that God "will bring them back to this place and let them live in safety."[33] I agree with Jeremiah. Through experience that has grown my trust and healed my perspective, I now know the Spirit truly is safe and good. The once-fearful little girl now experiences the presence, comfort, direction, conviction, and power of the One who loves so deeply.

---

[32] C.S. Lewis, *The Lion the Witch and the Wardrobe.*
[33] Jer. 32:37

Chapter 24

Scripture
Sheep Trust a Familiar Voice
by Phil Anderson

Phil Anderson is a father of three and an avid disc golf player. He is on staff with Journey as a program coordinator in Nova Scotia.

Back when I was younger—and fitter—I spent a summer working and living on a sheep farm. The owner of the farm woke up early each morning to do something a little odd; he would read his Bible (*ok, what's so special about that?*). He would read it out loud (*still not weird!*) to the sheep! (*huh?!? Why?*). He wasn't trying to convert the sheep or make them less "sheepy." He did it because he wanted them to recognize his voice. This is worth repeating and since it's the main point of this chapter, I'll say it again: *the shepherd wanted his sheep to recognise his voice.* He reasoned that the more he spoke to them, the more likely they would come to him when he called them from the field, and not be led astray by someone else who could try to steal them away.

Do you recognize God's voice when He speaks? The most important and reliable guide on our path is the Bible; it is often called The Word of God. The more we immerse ourselves in it, the more we will recognize God's voice. Lately, I've been thinking a lot about the phrase "This is what the Lord says…" It occurs 789 times in the Bible. That's a lot! And the phrase "Declares the Lord" occurs another 714 times. It's a miracle that the Creator of the universe would speak to humankind. The Bible could have been one page long with God abandoning His creation after the Fall in Genesis chapter three, but the whole of scripture is a testimony that God doesn't give up on us. It's a long conversation between a faithful God and a not-so-faithful people.

Our Bible-soaked minds and hearts can hear the Spirit more effectively and can discern the path of wisdom more reliably as we regularly open the Bible. But the Bible isn't just a list of God's sayings. The scriptures are a collection of all kinds of literature: history, poetry, prophecy, letters, and all written over 2,000 years ago and over a 1,500-year timespan by many authors. Its variety is a wonderful gift, a buffet with something for everyone. The Bible introduces us to people who have walked the path before us, with varying degrees of success, and they become, in a way, companions on the journey.

In a season of my life when I really wanted a mentor, I imagined I was Timothy to Paul and he was writing to me. I have also related to David, a songwriter like myself, who continued to engage with God even when he felt far from God or guilty due to sin. Both are emotional states I can find myself in as well. It's a wonder that David kept crying out to God, and even praising Him, in very difficult times. Ultimately, Scripture shows us how Jesus walked the path of obedience, remaining in God's delight.

Prayer that involves listening for God's voice is a key element of the Journey Discipleship Course. I believe God still speaks today, and I have experienced it myself as I pay attention and listen. That being said, a pitfall in listening prayer is looking for a new word from God without immersing ourselves in the timeless and timely word of God in the scriptures. We say to God "Speak to me," which is essentially saying, "Tell me something new," when in fact He has already spoken.

I am often guilty of wanting to hear something new from God. To correct this tendency, aside from slowly reading the scriptures, I try to come to Him in prayer asking, "Lord, is there something you have already told me that you want me to dwell on again?" I often turn to my old journals for guidance here. More often than not, there is a scripture passage He shows me that spoke to me in a difficult season. As I return to these passages, I ask myself: *What do you want me to know from this passage right now?* There is a richness and depth that emerges when we reflect and meditate on scripture. I hear His voice anew.

Here are a couple passages I return to frequently: "This is what the Sovereign LORD, the Holy One of Israel, says: In repentance and rest is your salvation, in quietness and trust is your strength,"[34] and "This is what the LORD says: 'Stand at the crossroads and look; ask for the ancient paths, ask where the good way is, and walk in it, and you will find rest for your souls.'"[35] Both of these passages are anchors for my soul, challenging my natural inclination to strive, seek new things, or work to be good. They remind me to slow down and to live out healthy rhythms in faith and life. Every time I meditate on these scriptures, the Lord has something for me. The timeless word of God written so long ago in another context, to another people group, becomes a timely word from God for me right now. I pray you also have passages like these as anchors for your soul.

But what about when the Bible feels dry or too familiar? I've sadly also been there before, more often than I'd like to admit. I sometimes wish I had a mountaintop experience every time I open my Bible, but it isn't so. In those times, I need to push through, trusting that a regular dose of the scriptures will consistently and slowly soak my mind. Likewise, when I am lacking in passion to be in God's word, I read, or listen to, people who are excited about Jesus and the scriptures until I become excited about them too. And it works! Passion is contagious.

---

[34] Isa. 30:15 NIV
[35] Jer. 6:16 NIV

There is no shame in letting someone else bring you to God's Word. It's like when the first disciples invited their friend or brother to Jesus. Andrew brought Peter, Philip brought Nathanael, the Samaritan woman brought the whole town. Jesus didn't reject them or shame them because they didn't come by their own initiative. And He won't reject you if you let another come alongside and bring you to Him and his word.

Those sheep back on the farm followed their shepherd's voice. He could calm a rambunctious flock in the pen with a word. God's word can have a calming effect, giving us a new perspective on our lives when anxiety rises. It can act like a movie soundtrack. Picture yourself watching a scary movie in a suspenseful moment: the bad guy could jump out at any moment... the music is eerie and getting louder... but then you push MUTE (which I do). What happens? It doesn't seem so scary, does it? What if you change the dark orchestral music to a bluegrass tune on banjo and harmonica? The moment wouldn't feel intimidating at all. What if listening to God's word regularly could change the atmosphere of our daily lives? It could change our scary moments like an argument with a spouse, an unexpected call from the doctor, job loss, or even a pandemic. It could then turn it into something less overwhelming because we are following the voice of the Shepherd, the Good Shepherd who brings us through the valley of the shadow of death as we recognize and follow His voice.[36]

There are many other voices out there: my own, the world's, and the evil one's. I want to recognise the voice of my Shepherd and the greatest way to do that is to read the time-tested book that repeatedly declares: *"This is what the Lord says..."*

---

[36] Ps. 23

Chapter 25

Together in Brokenness and Healing
by Graeme Lauber

It was the loud SNAP that let me know that something was wrong; ankles aren't supposed to make that noise. It turned out that this pleasant, apparently safe, little hike with friends had resulted in a couple of shattered bones needing surgery, plates, screws.

The healing process ended up taking months, and during my recovery, I needed a lot of help. I couldn't carry anything while I was on crutches; if I wanted a drink, or a book, or a computer, someone generally had to carry it for me. I learned to hop, but anyone who knows me knows I'm not really made for hopping. I'm more Clydesdale than rabbit—I like plenty of contact with the ground. This sometimes meant I had to throw my arm around the shoulder of a friend to get support as I hobbled around.

No one really knows who first said, "Church is not a museum for saints, but a hospital for sinners" but the analogy of church as hospital is certainly very old. Throughout my convalescence, I spent a fair amount of time at the hospital, and I noticed that in a hospital there are two basic types of people—healers and patients—the people who provide care, and the people who receive care. There are lots of different kinds of people around, but they are mostly trying to help—visiting patients, cleaning for patients, analyzing patients, treating patients—unless they are actually patients themselves. It's really all healers and patients.

So, when we say that church is like a hospital, we can think that church people are one of these; either healers or patients. If you're in ministry, or lead a small group, or teach kids, or lead worship, you will likely think of yourself as a healer. But you might also think of yourself as a patient, going to church to receive care.

Thinking about church this way has some problems. If you always come to church as a healer, you'll likely get some thanks and attention, but you will eventually find that, without some healing yourself, you run out of time, energy and patience. You'll burn out if you're always giving care and never receiving it. The attitude of a patient is even worse—a patient comes to church hoping for care, for great sermons, or lively worship, or loving community, and they're inevitably disappointed. There will always be bad sermons, offkey songs, and Sunday mornings when no one says hello.

I broke my ankle very close to the Canada/US border. I could have tried to hop to the hospital, but there were ten miles and an international border in the way. Being a Clydesdale, it's likely I would have crushed my remaining good leg. I needed help to get off the trail, help to cross the border, help to get into the emergency room, help to remember what happened while I was high on Ketamine, help, help, help for everything. I was the patient; others were the healers.

In our spiritual lives, when we first begin to look at our needs and recognize our wounds, we need a lot of help. We need people around us so we can throw our arm around their shoulders and keep the weight off our spiritually broken ankle. People who pray with us, pray for us, hear our confession, rebuke our shame, remind us that they love us, remind us that God loves us, celebrate our progress.

My ankle is a lot better now, but honestly, it still hurts a bit as I sit here at the computer (it's been about a year and a half), or when I use the stairs. I'm not sure if it will ever be 100%. This is also true of our spiritual wounds; they heal, but they probably won't be 100% until we meet Jesus. There likely will always be some pain, a bit of temptation, a certain longing. We will always find that we need some help, that there are days when the ankle simply won't bear the weight, and we need to throw our arm around someone's shoulder. We will always be patients, needing prayer, a listening ear, encouragement. But I have had some healing. If friend broke his ankle, he could throw his arm around my shoulder. I can do *some* of the praying, the listening, the encouraging. I can also be the healer.

It's tempting to think that this is the model—we don't have to be a patient *or* a healer, we could be a patient *and* a healer—some days we help, other days we receive help. But this doesn't get us out of the earlier problem. We end up simply switching between the roles—one role leads to burnout, the other leads to disappointment. There will be days—lots of days—when helping seems overwhelming, because our own wounds hurt, our own ankles ache; days when we can't respond to anyone needing our support. There will also be lots of days when we're hurting, needing to be patients, and we can't find anyone to help. When it comes to spirituality, the reality is that I don't just have a broken ankle—I have two broken legs, two broken arms, some cracked ribs and a serious heart problem. I am a mess, and so are you. We need better help than we can provide for ourselves.

So, the surprising truth is that the church is not doing its best when we try to help one another. We are not at our best when we encourage people to be healers, or patients, or to combine the roles of healer and patient. We are at our best when we point to better help. Our best work is to point past me and you, past ourselves, and on to Jesus. The church works when we say, "Go to Jesus for His help, and you will be amazed at what you can do. You'll be amazed at the wounds you can overcome, and the ways you'll be able to carry on in good health."

This means that when I'm in patient mode, I am throwing my arms around Jesus' shoulders; and when I am in doctor mode, I'm encouraging other people to throw their arms around Jesus' shoulders; and when I'm in REAL patient mode, I'm letting other people tell me to throw my arms around Jesus' shoulders. Because it's all about Jesus, beginning, middle, and end.

With Jesus, I can walk, even when I'm wounded, not because I'm able to bear my weight, but because He is.

Chapter 26

A Sitcom Uncovers Something Deeper
by Phil Anderson

When I was in university, I had an acquaintance who loved the show "Friends." She really got into the show; if it was on TV in the student lounge, we all had to stop everything and watch quietly. Once, she even became teary-eyed during an episode and said, "I wish my friends were like that." My buddies and I laughed, but in all honesty, we also desired more from our friendships, but we wouldn't have admitted it. We wanted good friends.

That was all before Facebook. Now I have tons of friends. 948 to be exact. You may think "Wow, that's a lot!" or maybe, "Less than 1,000?!? This guy needs to network more." In 2018, the *Wall Street Journal* published a piece with a blaring headline "The Loneliest Generation," claiming that we are a generation with the most "friends" ever, but we are actually the loneliest people to have lived... ever.[37] When I look at my life, I can see this to be true. With all those "friends" online, I still feel quite lonely.

Friendship can be treated very lightly in our society, but they can be the most significant relationships in our lives. My friend in university wished her friends were more like the ones on TV. How would you describe a good friend? One who calls instead of texts?

---

[37] Janet Adamy and Paul Overberg. "The loneliest generation: Americans, more than ever, are aging alone" *The Wall Street Journal*. (December 11, 2018) https://www.wsj.com/articles/the-loneliest-generation-americans-more-than-ever-are-aging-alone-11544541134

Who is vulnerable instead of just talking about the weather? Who prays with you instead of just giving advice? This sounds like a good friend to me. I could look at this list and think: "I wish my friends were like that." Or I could ask myself a better question: "Have I been a friend like that?" And to be honest, I have often not been a good friend. I have often been selfish in my friendships or guarded and self-protecting. When they asked, "Hey, how are things?" my answer was, "Fine," while I was far from feeling fine.

Why is friendship so hard? In my experience, there are a few reasons, but two especially stand out. First, it's hard because it's important. Nothing important and good is easy, and that includes friendship. Second, it's hard because we are all broken people and our brokenness can create friction points when we get close to others. It can be easier to hide and keep people at a distance, but then I miss out on the sharpening that comes from getting close to another person. "As iron sharpens iron, so one person sharpens another."[38]

Why is it important to have good friends? It is important because we need to hear from Jesus and we sometimes hear best from Jesus through good friends. I love how Bonhoeffer puts it in the wonderfully short book *Life Together*: "[a Christian] needs his brother [and his sister] solely because of Jesus Christ. The Christ in his own heart is weaker than the Christ in the word of his brother; his own heart is uncertain, his brother's is sure."[39] My heart is often too critical or too lenient on myself while the words of Christ from a brother or sister bring light and accuracy. I can't count how many times I've either justified sinful behaviour or wallowed in shame because of a passing thought. It was only when I heard accurately from a friend that I could walk again in the light.

---

[38] Prov. 27:17 NIV

[39] Dietrich Bonhoeffer, *Life Together* (1939).

I am fortunate to have a good friend and I hear from Jesus often through him. God gave him to me in my 30s. He initiated that we meet once a month as accountability partners and that moved toward many shared experiences, like racquetball games to 3-day hikes in the woods. Even in this season of COVID-19, when I felt unmotivated to initiate with people, he would call me up and invite me for walks. He would open up first about his struggles and ask me to pray for him. He makes me want to be more like Jesus, or at least a better version of myself, without ever giving me advice on how to do so. He simply models it. Even as I write this, I look forward to our next walk together.

I have a couple other friends who I meet with bi-weekly via video chat to connect and pray for each other. Even these long-distance relationships are important and life-giving. I look forward to them as well.

Maybe you feel you don't have any good friends and are unsure where to start. You may tell yourself, "I'm not a good conversationalist; I don't know how to speak Jesus' words to others." I tell you the same thing I tell myself almost daily, "Don't try to be interesting, just be interested." My reluctance to connect with new people usually comes from this unhelpful expectation that I need to be interesting for people to like me. I think I need something interesting to say. Instead, I want to focus on asking good questions and listening well. Be a close friend and you'll get a close friend. "Do not forsake your friend."[40] It's a simple idea, but it really changes how we interact with people.

What if people don't want to be our friends? What if we have difficulty making good, lasting friendships? This can be very painful, but here is a reminder that we who are in Jesus have a different, more constant source of friendship. We have a friend who

---

[40] Prov. 27:10

will never forsake us or cast us out: Jesus Christ.[41] May that be an anchor for your soul as you befriend those around you, especially those in the family of God.

The best friends are those who are anchored in their love from another source. It keeps them from overstepping boundaries. Until we have that reliable source of a Friend, we crave something from others that they cannot possibly fulfill. "You can pick your friends, you can pick your nose, but you shouldn't pick your friend's nose" (George Carlin). This may sound silly or obvious, however, there is a lot of truth in this statement. Friends are people who we choose, and who accompany us on our journey. They likely lack the complexity and burden of a romantic or spousal relationship or the obligations and baggage of family connections. Friendship can provide us with intimacy and connection with people who are freely chosen and companions on the journey.

However, our friendships are healthiest when they have boundaries. In chapter six of Paul's letter to the Galatians, he first speaks of carrying each other's burdens and this fulfills the law, but then in verse five he speaks of each carrying their own load.[42] Healthy friendships have boundaries where people don't overstep their independence nor seek for them to fulfill an unmet need.
Friendship is still something I am growing in. I am thankful for those friends God has brought on my path. And I pray that I will be a good friend to others. One who is interested instead of interesting. One who calls instead of texts. One who is vulnerable instead of just talking about the weather. And one who prays with you instead of just giving advice.

Lord, thank you for calling us your friends. Help us to receive your affection and delight. Help us to be good friends, unafraid of going deep with others; we can only do this well by remaining in your love and friendship.

---

[41] John 6:37, John 15:15
[42] Gal. 6:2,5

Chapter 27

Singing with an Unchosen Choir
by Stephanie Robinson

Stephanie Robinson is a passionate teacher and mother of four, who delights to come alongside people in their walk of faith. Based in Halifax, Nova Scotia, she has been on staff with Journey since 2016.

The clanking dishes and swishing of water was accompanied by the sweet sounds of the three inter-weaving parts of *Dona Nobis Pacem*. It was Sunday afternoon and, after hosting church newcomers for Sabbath dinner, we were singing together as we did the dishes. These Latin words, *Dona Nobis Pacem*, are a prayer asking God to grant us peace. Family singing usually brought a measure of peace when an undesirable chore needed to be done, or arguing and grumpiness needed to be kept at bay.

My dad often initiated singing as a way of centering us on Jesus, lifting our focus from whatever tiresome task was at hand and instead connecting us with the satisfaction of beautiful harmony and lyrics of praise. Music was a thread that tied our family together. We often sang grace in four-part harmony before we began the evening meal or sang rounds on long car trips to prevent bickering and complaining about the lack of air-conditioning and uncomfortable seats.

But music became not only something that bonded our family together. It also became an illustration of both the challenges and joys of life together. Singing harmony was like the beauty of expressing our own personalities and strengths and weaknesses and having them complement each other. But music, for me, also highlighted comparison, competition, the mask of perfectionism, dissonance, and judgement.

My journey with music highlights my struggle with my identity and how that affected my relationship with my family. As a middle child between two highly gifted siblings, I often felt I couldn't measure up in areas of education, deep philosophical discussions, and spiritual matters, and so I spent many years thinking that God's call on my life was somehow less than the call on my sister and brother's lives. Since I loved to sing and play the piano, I worked hard to prove myself in music, competing in many festivals and winning scholarships and eventually studying music at university.

I looked to music to give me significance and to try to prove my worth. I looked to music to *be* my identity rather than realizing that my God-given melody could only be sung as I learned how to embrace my true identity as a beloved daughter of God.

It has been a long journey for me to learn to joyfully embrace the melody that God has asked me to sing and watch the beautiful way that He weaves my line together with the lines of my parents and brother and sister and my husband and each of my four children. But as I have learned to rest more in the singing of my own line, I have come to recognize other important lessons about family life that are illustrated through music.

First of all, I've learned that each melodic line must serve the whole. Sometimes the alto or tenor line can be very repetitive or uninteresting to sing, but each note is important to complete the sound of the full chord—to serve the greater whole. In the same way, each person in a family unit will have a different call on his or her life, a different set of strengths and weaknesses and a different role to play in the family unit. Just as the apostle Paul talks about the different roles within the family of God, we will also have different parts to play in our family units.

Time spent in the Journey courses and with Journey staff were significant in helping me recognize that God had given me my own melodic line to sing and that it was no less important than the lines that He had asked my brother and sister to sing. I spent too many years comparing myself to them and failing to measure up in my own mind. But each of us was called to serve the greater good, to faithfully sing our own melodic lines for the beauty and blessing of the whole family unit, the wider family of God and the salvation of the world.

Secondly, music helped me make the discovery that the richest and the most satisfying harmony comes after dissonance. Holding the note that doesn't belong in the chord builds tension and anticipation for the sweetness of resolution. In the same way, after harsh words, unfair judgements and the ache of being misunderstood, the family bonds often grew stronger and deeper if we resolved the discord and practiced asking for and receiving forgiveness. But there were times, as in any family unit, that misunderstanding or resentment prevailed and got buried, having to wait until adult years to examine and pray through the memories and feelings that surfaced.

With my own children, there have been lines of bubbly laughter and celebration of milestones, followed by stretches filled with dissonance that make my heart ache. Attempting family togetherness does not often turn out the way I hope it will; words are said that I wish would not be said and criticism, comparison and complaining rear their ugly heads. But, on a discouraging day, my pastor once told me, "You are honouring God by faithfully continuing to attempt togetherness." So, we continue to prioritize family meals, long chats, playing together and working together. And I try to remember to thank God that when the ugly things of the heart are exposed, they can be brought to the cross for healing. Being broken and authentic is better than looking perfect. Both chordal and clashing notes bring color to the whole song, reflecting the way God uses both our struggles and joys to weave the tapestries of our lives.

Thirdly, I learned that, when we each sing our part, making the glory of God our goal, the notes and phrases that are the weakest for us are somewhat buoyed up by the strength of the other parts. We were not intended to live in isolation and be under the constant pressure and vulnerability of "singing solo." We were created to live in community, but if I'm trying to make my line stand out, I've lost sight of the fact that this song is all about Jesus, and we were created to sing together.

The melody that Jesus came to sing was the song of the Father's love for the world. The whole song of Scripture is this melody of God's heart to restore all people to harmony with him—to bring back reconciliation and shalom. Jesus didn't grasp at His identity, nor did He compare and compete and cling to equality with His Father. Jesus knew who He was and so he was able to faithfully sing the Father's song of love to the world, in a way that the world could recognize the true heart of the triune God.

How can we participate in this song of love and shalom? This question reminds me of Mother Teresa's famous rhetorical question, "What can you do to promote world peace? Go home and love your family." Two significant ways that my parents loved us was through giving us the gift of music and introducing us to Jesus' song of love and peace.

Part of my coming home journey has been about learning to sing, with all my heart, the line that God has given me to sing as I settle deeper into my identity as the Father's beloved girl. The strain and dissonance lessen as I stop competing and comparing with other melodies. Out of this place, I can more effectively love my family and teach my own children to sing the vastly unique melodies that God has given each one of them to sing. But, by God's grace, I pray they will learn to sing as part of the whole, to bring glory to God and beautiful music to the world.

Chapter 28

A Bookish Mind meets a Craving Heart
by Fred DeVries

Fred DeVries lives in London, Ontario, with his wife and two sons. He served on the national team of Journey Canada in Vancouver for 10 years, and edited the first major revision of the ministry's discipleship material.

The summer before heading off to university, my pastor gave me a book. I cannot remember its title or its content. But I do remember the Scripture verse he wrote on the opening page: "Be warned, my son... of making many books there is no end, and much study wearies the body."[43]

In sharing this verse, I believe my pastor meant well. But I took some offence to the admonishment about the endlessness of writing and studying. I loved learning. I loved school. Diving into a book to uncover new ideas, new places and new experiences was a sanctuary during my childhood and teenage years. I would even read encyclopedias, or more accurately, get sidetracked in my research and end up delving into all sorts of topics unrelated to my homework.

I grew up in a Reformed household. Not a reformatory, although it might have seemed that way at times, but a home where my parents lived out Reformed theology. That meant, for me anyway, obeying strict rules of conduct, studying doctrine in catechism

---

[43] Eccles. 12:12

class, and memorizing biblical teaching. Books and study became my refuge.

By the time I started university, I knew a lot about what it meant to be Reformed. What the Bible taught. What God wanted from me.

Yet, I never truly knew the Father. I understood the Bible. I read about God. My mind contained a lot of knowledge *about* Him, but my heart held little experience *of* Him.

In my broken attempt to be whole by reading books and studying doctrine, I prayed for God to take away my pain and abuse and to heal my identity. From what I absorbed through my church and family, I believed this was the only way for God to work in my life.

He never answered my prayer—at least, not in the way I wanted.

Participating in the Journey Canada program brought me to a place where no book or study would save and heal me from my hurt. Slowly, as my hard shell cracked open, I experienced Jesus in a strangely new way. My armour of knowledge was stripped away and replaced by His intense love. My bookish mind finally met my craving heart.

Nearly 25 years have passed since those Jesus experiences. Many more have come since then. And I'm sure many more are yet to come. Through it all, I've tried to live a more balanced life of heart and mind. I still read and study (not as much as I used to because I'm a father to two boys!), but I do so with a healthy appetite to experience Him through the words on the page.

I've gravitated to books where life and knowledge, heart and mind are intertwined. Rather than reading the hard truth of doctrine, I sought out mediative authors who wrote reflective books where the Christian life is painted in greys, not in blacks and whites.

From the gentle words of Henri Nouwen: "It is not easy to stay with your loneliness. The temptation is to nurse your pain or to escape into fantasies about people who will take it away. When you can acknowledge your loneliness in a safe, contained place, you make your pain available for God's healing."[44]

From the simply profound writings of Dietrich Bonhoeffer: "In confession, a person breaks through to certainty."[45]

From the meditative movements of Frederick Buechner: "Where do you look for the home you long for if not to the irrecoverable past? How do you deal with...that longing for whatever the missing thing is that keeps even the home of the present from being true home?"[46]

From the sublime musings of Ann Lamott: "You know you have created God in your own image when it turns out He hates the same people you do."[47]

From the pastoral thoughts of A.W. Tozer: "It is probably impossible to think without words, but if we permit ourselves to think with the wrong words, we shall soon be entertaining erroneous thoughts; for words, which are given us for the expression of thought, have a habit of going beyond their proper bounds."[48]

In my youth, books became my unhealthy shelter, a place to disappear from the realness of the Father. While giving me a foundation of faith, bookish doctrine and theology kept me from His presence.

---

[44] Henri Nouwen, *The Inner Voice of Love* (2014).

[45] Dietrich Bonhoeffer, *Life Together* (1939).

[46] Frederick Buechner, *The Longing for Home: Recollections and Reflections* (2009).

[47] Anne Lamott, *Traveling Mercies: Some Thoughts on Faith* (2006).

[48] A. W. Tozer, *The Knowledge of the Holy.*

Yet, by walking through a painful healing journey where He revealed Himself as the living and gracious Word, I discovered books and writings allow me to enter new spaces of hope and rest. I guess, in some ways, books have become the bookends of my life.

Chapter 29

A Heart Opens to a Worthy Companion
by Ron Brookman

Ron Brookman is an active contemplative who lives in Sydney, Australia. He served on the inaugural Journey Global board.

For the first 30 years of my Christian walk I presented myself as a "good boy." The inner fight against my father's "bad boy" label, and the mask I constructed to hide my shame, sexuality and addiction, led to a theology and spirituality of perfection. Effort to be a "victorious overcomer" stole the stillness needed to discover intimacy with God. My prayer life was based on denial of my brokenness. Frantic work and stubborn pride made fellowship with the saints shallow. Missing this very heart of the gospel of grace, I also missed authentic fellowship with the saints, and the gifts, challenges, reproofs, and encouragement they bring.

Self-Protection
It's not an exaggeration to say I quaked at the thought of approaching my closest mate with my heart's deepest dilemma. We both pastored an inner-city church. Con, my assistant lay-pastor, was a saint whom I regarded far more gifted and mature than I, a man with a true servant heart. His humility would not have made the comparison. I was the "senior" pastor, by ordination only. A year older than Con, I lagged behind him in spiritual wisdom, experience, and gifting. And I struggled. Weighed down by untamed sexual desire that had progressed to an addictive cycle, I secretly binged in anonymous encounters every four months or so.

I yearned to unburden myself to my friend, but suspecting that he would not understand, instead calling me to surrender my ministry and therefore my livelihood, reputation, and desperately-clung-to identity, I resisted. To be vulnerable to him was a risk too costly. Whenever I considered exposing my cry and heart to him, I would see righteousness beaming through him, reflecting the piercing flame that gleams through the eyes of our ascended Lord.[49] Very scary to my "survival."

I remained hidden in secrecy, God's mercy my only hope. But Jesus' eyes would eventually pierce me through other saints, and finally in a most merciful way, through Con.

Vulnerability
Several years of fear and shame yielded to a desperate boldness to confess to David, the pastor of another church. He became my confidant and prayerful counsellor who fortnightly heard the confessions of my slow journey to freedom. David patiently walked with me over three years, helping me lay hold of grace to break addiction, and to find a deep measure of healing and of release. He was the saint who reflected the mercy and healing in those Eyes of Fire, described in Revelation 1:14.

Four years later I decided to walk further in light and confess the hidden sin of my first eight years of ministry to the church. Understandably, Con and the elders were shocked by my revelations. Con explained to me that, though I had found victory over my sin, the leaders who had trusted me to call me to ministry initially and then pray, work, and fellowship with me for twelve years, no longer knew who I was. My mask had hidden the real me. They felt they only knew the mask. As a matter of discipline, they asked me to stand aside for some months, as much for me to receive counselling as for them to work through the shock and to discern the best way forward for the church. It was a painful but

---

[49] Revelation 1:14

necessary time. Not just *my* pain, but also that of Ruth, my wife, and of course of Con, the elders and other saints in the church. Con again represented the consuming fire in Jesus' eyes!

Five months later I was conditionally restored to ministry. But my ministerial mojo seemed lost. I struggled for a few months, then resigned, not knowing where the Lord would lead.
Faithfully, He led us to an internship at Desert Stream Ministries in California, where I met Toni and Mardi Dolfo-Smith, who brought great encouragement and wisdom. Returning to Australia, I was called to lead Living Waters Ministry nationally. Over the next decade Con opened his home and his heart to me. We would meet for mutual encouragement, prayer and some good laughs. He proved to be the affirming link from those years of ministry which had ended in shame and apparent failure. He affirmed my ongoing call to ministry, was a sign of forgiveness from the past, and a great encouragement of hope for the future.

Through our life's journey, God provides accompanying saints for the long haul. They help us reflect over the past and give perspective to our ongoing journey. Jesus' fire-filled eyes still looked upon me through Con, now more as eyes of mercy, bringing light to my path rather than the purifying fire of discipline and truth. I enjoyed our times together, being able to simply be who I was, failure and all, not having to pretend anything other, being totally accepted for my journey. How healing!

The Glory of the Saints Shines through Shadows
Saints are those whom God has called, adopted and set apart to inherit His Kingdom. We are holy because the Lord dwells within us, individually and communally. We are fitted together as living stones in the spiritual temple He is building. Saints bring different gifts and different facets of the face, eyes and heart of Jesus to one another. Because none of us reflects every part of the Person of Jesus, and because each of us is still putting to death our flesh, the light of the Lord shines through saints' shadows. We walk in

weakness. As the bumper sticker said, "Christians aren't perfect, just forgiven."

God chose another saint to open my heart further to His healing grace. I never met him nor spoke with him. In fact, he had passed to glory by the time his legacy lit my path. My dear friend, and knock-about-saint, Cam Rimmer, encouraged me to read Henri Nouwen, a Catholic priest, professor, prolific author and theologian, who died in 1996. His was *a spirituality of imperfection*. In volume after volume, Nouwen stressed the fact that it was through our weakness, struggles, vulnerability, brokenness, and suffering, indeed our very sinfulness when confessed, that we find true communion with God. He wrote about finding peace and wholeness "in our weakness, in those places of our hearts where we feel most broken, most insecure, most in agony, most afraid."[50] Fellowship through the Cross of Jesus brings us into union with the Father, who calls and embraces us as *His Beloved*. Nouwen helped me surrender false perfection, to be perfectly embraced as God's *beloved*, weak and broken as I was. Reflecting on this saint's writings helped me slow down to find the peace to surrender those strongholds of my heart, in turn to encounter true fellowship with the saints.

In the Creeds, Christians confess our belief in the Communion of Saints. This fellowship spans the millennia, joining us to the life of Jesus lived through the individuals of His Church. We encounter the saints in the church circles we mix in, but we can also be enriched by the saints who have gone before. They leave such a rich heritage, as Nouwen did for me. Mysteriously, the living temple the Lord is building with the living stones of the saints, spans all history, every nation and tongue, and every expression of *church*, the home of earthbound saints. Still greater, however, is the number of those who have ascended to glory, who still encourage

---

[50] Henri Nouwen, *Finding My Way Home: Pathways to Life and the Spirit* (2001).

us in our faith and mission. Hebrews 12:1 reminds us that we are surrounded by their encouragement.

Growing Together in Love, to Know *Love*

Some years ago, my friend Con was diagnosed with liver cancer. Knowing that death was conquered, that he was going to join Jesus and those saints in glory, he lived fully to his final day here. Inviting his friends to visit in his last month, he sat, physically weak on his hospice bed, but with divine strength, to speak words of life to each of us. He prayed individual blessings upon everyone who visited. The love in his eyes enabled the furious flames of love in Jesus' eyes to shine upon us!

Paul prayed in Ephesians that as saints *together* we would come to comprehend the width, length, height and depth of God's love, high above the realms of this world's knowledge.[51] We can't do that apart from one another. At times our fellowship will be sweet indeed. At other times saints will rub like sandpaper, whether through personality, brokenness, words which wound our pride or bring correction. Heeded, they bring healing. Saints have a function to cross-fertilise each other's journeys towards holiness, helping us grow into Jesus' fullness. Love is the mortar between the saints in the spiritual temple the Lord is building and indwelling. Side by side we grow and work together in love, patiently giving, forgiving, accepting, encouraging, and building up one another, as Jesus delights in us, and fully forms Himself in us.

---

[51] Eph. 3:18

Section 5—The Road

Our family enjoys the occasional hike, and living in Calgary means we are in one of the best hiking areas in the world. We have a lot of different options within a few hours' drive of our house. If we want something gentle, we can head east to take a walk in prairie grassland, alongside creeks or rivers, or explore the Martian landscape of the Alberta Badlands. North and south of us are wetlands, with interesting birds and other wildlife. The real prize, however, is to the west and the Canadian Rockies. The hiking is much more challenging, but there are glacial streams, waterfalls, and incredible views. The smell of the air alone will extend your life by ten years.

In this section, we want to consider one final aspect of our journey—the actual road upon which we walk. In an era of cars and pavement, we don't often think about the significance of the road beneath us, but when we are hiking, we know that the path makes a big difference. Is it steep? Is it rocky? Is the view worth it?

In our spiritual lives, the path we walk is really the path of prayer. Some people can find this discouraging, since prayer is not something that comes easily for them, but this may be in part due to the fact that their view of prayer and the forms it can take is not large enough. This can be partly to do with the church where we grew up—I grew up in a tradition that believed extemporaneous prayer was the way to go and was very suspicious of pre-written or set prayers. Others may have grown up in more liturgical churches and not feel comfortable with speaking their own thoughts in their own words. But just like there are many hikes available in my region, there are many ways we can approach the life of prayer. Some will require a bit of discipline and may feel uncomfortable, but may bring us to places of previously unimagined beauty. Others will be easier or more natural and will be able to sustain us for the long haul.

In the chapters that follow we will read a bit about how to position ourselves in a prayerful attitude—to find ways to make prayer easier for ourselves. We will also explore a few prayer practices that people have found helpful. Our travels together will end with a meditation on "thin places" and the way God truly connects with His creation.

-GL

"Lord, Teach Us to Pray" by Paul Spilsbury - Watercolour

Prayer (I)

Prayer the church's banquet, angel's age,
God's breath in man returning to his birth,
The soul in paraphrase, heart in pilgrimage,
The Christian plummet sounding heav'n and earth
Engine against th' Almighty, sinner's tow'r,
Reversed thunder, Christ-side-piercing spear,
The six-days world transposing in an hour,
A kind of tune, which all things hear and fear;
Softness, and peace, and joy, and love, and bliss,
Exalted manna, gladness of the best,
Heaven in ordinary, man well drest,
The milky way, the bird of Paradise,
Church-bells beyond the stars heard, the soul's blood,
The land of spices; something understood.

- George Herbert

Chapter 30

Prayer is the Road We Walk
by Dan Heavenor

Dan Heavenor is a spiritual director, retreat leader, and bus driver. He has volunteered with Journey for 20 years. He lives in North Vancouver, British Columbia with Andrea.

"Lord, Teach Us to Pray"

Have you ever wondered what prompted the disciples to ask this question of Jesus? As Jews they were already well acquainted with prayer. They heard and spoke prayers all the time, in synagogue, at home. What do you think they saw in Jesus that provoked this question? I believe their question came from a deep longing to be connected to God. In Luke 11, where this question arises, Jesus had been praying and, upon finishing, the disciples asked their question. They were hearing something in Jesus' relationship to his Father they wanted in on.

I want in on that, too, but prayer has often been a struggle. I am easily distracted. I have far too little discipline. And my desire for God can easily drain out in the wake of life's busyness. Is there a way to understand prayer that might stoke my longings rather than my despair? I believe so.

Jesus Prays

Prayer does not begin with us. It always begins with God. In a course on prayer, Eugene Peterson began by stating in no uncertain terms, "The most important thing to know about prayer is this: Jesus prays."[52] Prayer begins with Him. When I think about prayer, I automatically think about me. What am I supposed to do? What am I supposed to say? We think of prayer as words and thoughts and perhaps even actions that we initiate. If we think about God at all it is usually whether or not He is going to give us what we want.

Still, Jesus prays. We learn in Hebrews 7:25 that Jesus always lives to intercede for us. Romans 8 also tells us that Jesus, as well as the Spirit, is interceding for us. There is a divine conversation going on within the Trinity about you! And what are they saying? Among many other things, Scripture tells us the Spirit prays within you, "Abba, Father."[53] This is the cry for intimacy, the longing to know oneself as beloved of God. And Jesus? "Not my will but yours, Father, be done."[54] This is the prayer of obedience, the courage to lay down one's life to follow God. I, for one, am not good at praying either of these prayers, much less living them, but they are already being prayed within me, and you, by God himself. God invites us to join him.

Prayer is the place where we engage with God, where we pay attention to God and say "Yes" to the offer of friendship with God. Prayer is the means by which we live our life before God. We begin by saying prayers. Over time prayer begins to escape the boundaries of "morning devotions" in order to run free through our entire day. Prayer begins to seep into our bones. The longer we live our lives with a growing awareness of God's loving presence, the more prayer becomes a posture rather than an activity. I no

---

[52] Eugene H Peterson. "Jesus Prays." *Prayer: Biblical Foundations.* (Lecture, 1994).

[53] Rom. 8:15, Gal. 4:6

[54] Matt. 26:39

longer strive to "seek God" in prayer. Thomas Merton says it this way: "Prayer does not consist in an effort to get across to God but in opening our eyes to see that we are already there."[55] The conversation is already happening and we are invited in.

But What Do I Do?

What does our "Yes" to God in prayer look like? Perhaps you have heard the phrase, "We learn to pray by praying." We begin where we are. There are no experts in prayer, no special skills required. We are all children reaching up with both arms hoping that Mom or Dad will lift us up. Prayer is a posture of desire. It is the articulation, sometimes with words, of our longings for our true home.

This posture begins with listening. If prayer is friendship, then attentive listening is required. I have a friend who is a fantastic listener and it is beyond healing to receive the gift of close attention as I attempt to share my heart. We have the opportunity in prayer to offer this gift to our Father. Before you jump ahead with all your needs and questions, take a moment to pause and listen first, "Here I am, Lord. I'm listening." What is on God's heart as you come to Him today? What are His desires, His pain, His joy that He might want to share with you? Scripture is the primary place where we hear God's heart, so praying with scripture is a basic way to listen to the Father.

For me, this often looks like placing myself into Gospel stories and paying attention to Jesus. When God speaks, He is not primarily giving us information or instructions. God's Word is a Person. God's primary "instruction" to us is the offer of friendship. Everything else follows from that. Watching Jesus is one way to listen to God's word.

---

[55] Cited in David Steindl-Rast, *Gratefulness: The Heart of Prayer* (1984).

Then, we respond. We offer who we are to the Lord. This means that we allow God into every nook and cranny of our hearts. This requires us to know what these nooks and crannies are, which we often do not. Lots of them we do not want to know. We hide them from God by never bringing them to the surface of our minds. But the gift of Jesus' intercession is that all of this is already part of the conversation. He sees every failure and source of shame already, and He loves us right in those places. As God did with Adam, He continues to call, "Where are you?" He desires for us to come out of hiding and open ourselves to Him that we might receive the love we so desperately need. I have discovered that I need other people in my life to accompany me in my prayers at this point. My shame is often too well hidden. I need friends to help call it into the light.

In our response to God, we bring all of our emotions, all our frustrations, our hopes, our failures, our anger. God has given you the ability to feel all that you are feeling. Living before Him means bringing all of this to prayer. God receives it as a gift. This is richer fare for prayer than any amount of pious language. God wants to hear your real self, not the "performing" self we often bring to prayer. If prayer bores you, and I admit that I can often be bored in prayer, then it might be an indication that you are not offering your real self. The conversation is stuck on talking about the weather, so to speak, and that's boring. Your boredom is an invitation to risk a new level of honesty in prayer.

Challenges in Prayer
Let's be honest, prayer has its challenges. We can fall into the trap of thinking if we pray the "right" way then God will answer us. We begin to think of prayer primarily in terms of method or technique. This can appear in very subtle ways. We think we have to use the right words, to be sincere enough, to have enough faith or be in some position of leadership. All of this points to a misunderstanding of the spiritual life that privileges strength over weakness. If we are strong in our praying, we think, then God will hear us. But we are not strong. We come as we are, weak, frail,

needy, treating God not like a slot machine but as a friend who has already been praying for us.

If we have been on a healing journey, we can find ourselves falling into another subtle trap, making demands upon God. In our desire for healing and wholeness our prayers have been prayers of asking for help, asking for healing, asking for rescue—and rightly so. God tells us to bring our needs to Him. But we can begin thinking that this is the entire extent of prayer. We can begin expecting things of God, coming to God in order to get something and then being frustrated when we do not receive it. We all are guilty of this. I have learned to ask myself in the face of such feelings, "Do I want this thing more than I want Jesus? Is Jesus alone enough for me?"

The flip side of this challenge is resignation in prayer. Not wanting to make demands upon God we give up asking altogether. "God is going to do what he is going to do," we think, "so why pray at all?" I am very susceptible to this particular challenge. I can fear being disappointed. I fear placing my hope in something only to be turned away. That wound can still be very tender in me. But Scripture tells us to bring our prayers, ask our questions, wrestle it out with God. He named his people Israel which means "wrestling with God." God is looking for real people to engage with. There is growth in this struggle, especially when it forces us to face all the reasons why we are tempted to give up in prayer.

And finally, perhaps the greatest challenge of all, we are not good at prayer. We do not have the discipline, or the desire, or the attention. We look at others, perhaps, and long for their prayer life, not realizing that they, too, often feel a failure in prayer. To this Jesus responds, "Blessed are the poor in spirit."[56] God is not looking for eloquent pray-ers. He is not looking for people to reach some milestone of hours prayed each day. He wants you, however you come. One author describes our prayers as so much "groping

---

[56] Matt. 5:3

in the dark." Paul himself admits in Romans 8:26, "We do not know what to pray for."

Any "success" we may have, any consolation we may experience in prayer is pure gift. To be human is to be in need and perhaps nowhere is our need more evident than in our (in)ability to pray. But we take heart. When faced with a similar sense of not knowing what to do or where to go, Jesus' friend Thomas asked, "How can we know the way?" to which Jesus responds, to Him and to us, "I am the way, follow me."[57]

---

[57] John 14:5-6

Chapter 31

Greeted with a Goofy Smile
by Kirsten Rumary

Kirsten Rumary works for Journey Canada as the program resource coordinator and does spiritual direction in her spare time. She has the two funnest jobs in the whole world.

I grew up in a church community that was rooted in strong Biblical teaching. I remember being captivated by sermons where the pastor would explain the meaning of Scripture, opening up its mysteries. And I remember the animated conversations of my parents and their friends as they dug deep into the Word at their weekly Bible study. Something came alive for me, even as a young child, and I just knew that God was real.

However, I don't recall anyone specifically modelling how to engage God in conversation. Certainly, I heard grownups pray, but what I learned was that prayer looked and sounded a lot like talking *at* God—sort of like a one-way message left on someone's answering machine (readers born after 1990 may need to search the Interweb to understand this reference). So, I would dial up God, assuming He was far too busy saving the world to take my call, and I would leave my message (usually asking Him to take away sinful feelings and make me a better person). And then I'd hang up and hope He'd get the message and grant my request from afar.

A Journey Discipleship Course (JDC) was the place that modelled something different to me. Something new. There I was taught how to listen for God *in the moment*, to "hold the phone" so to speak, and wait for God to respond to me. And I discovered (surprise, surprise) that God had been waiting for me to do just that. He was on the line, anticipating me; He wanted to hear from me, and He had things to say. Intimate things.

From the opening pages of Scripture, we read that our God is a communicating God. He speaks the world into being. He walks and talks with the first humans in the Garden of Eden.[58] Even after the fall, God continues to speak to individuals and the prophets throughout the Old Testament. He even speaks through a donkey to get His point across![59] Here and there we notice He likes to mix it up a bit and communicate beyond words, through imagery in dreams and visions.[60] Then God comes to earth in the person of Jesus and speaks to people face-to-face again. And when Jesus leaves to return to His Father (and our Father), He says He will send an Advocate who will teach us and remind us of all we need to know.[61] There is a promise that the gift of the Presence of God is going to continue speaking to us through the Holy Spirit.

And that was the part that was missing for me: God *continues speaking*. To me personally. Uniquely. I didn't get that part. I knew God in His canonical box only. I still remember the first time He stepped off the page and became real to me. Early on in the JDC, my small group leader invited our group to imagine holding out our hearts to Jesus. "Hmm. This is new. Let's give it a shot." As I closed my eyes, I saw my heart in my imagination right away. It was black and oily, oozing nasty grossness. I was dismayed by the state of it; I couldn't bear to look. I felt before I saw two hands gently cover mine, resting on my heart. When I dared another look, I saw they were Jesus' hands because they had holes in them. Then, as His

---

[58] Gen. 3:8-10

[59] Num. 22:28-31

[60] Gen. 37:5-10, Dan. 2

[61] John 14:26

hands withdrew, I was blinded by the light of many diamonds, spilling through my fingers.

My heart was dazzling! In that simple exchange, Jesus demonstrated He saw my heart altogether differently than I did. And even though no words were used (no words were used!) I sensed the question posed: would I choose to accept He had the power, and obviously the desire, to transform me and my reality? I don't remember responding with words (no words!), just laughter. I laughed, and laughed, and laughed. In some musty old church basement, I had an *encounter* in real-time with the Living God who wanted to speak to me, and wanted to hear from me, no words required. I had grown up in church; that night, I became a believer.

Encounter. It's what we long for; it's what *we were made for*. From the time of our debut on the world stage way back in the Garden of our origin, we human creatures opened our eyes to the face of our Creator looking back at us. We woke up to a relationship. And when we pause in prayer now long enough to listen—when we turn off our favourite programs and put down our devices and shut out the noise and distraction of all the voices clamoring for our attention, "Look over here, buy our product that will surely make you feel alive and like you matter..."—we make space for encounter with God to happen.

Space. In any relationship, in any really good conversation or connection, space is needed for it to unfold and blossom. When we are busy, busy, busy, rushing about in all our very important busy business, filling, filling, filling up time, we miss opportunities for encounter and conversation with God to happen.

It's like a story my mom was telling me the other day about my 18-month-old nephew. He comes to visit her every week, and they have a little routine where they nap together (because apparently grandmas need naps just as much as toddlers do). My mom is usually up before him and so she lies there, watching him sleeping, waiting for him to wake up. And when he does, when he becomes aware of her looking at him, he grins at her. And then she grins back. They just lay there, grinning at each other like a couple of goofballs. Because they can. Nothing is expected of my nephew. Nothing demanded. My mom would be content to lie there for hours, smiling back at his little face.

I love that story, because I know the players and I think it's hilarious, but also because I wonder if God isn't kind of like that? I have this suspicion that He's hanging around, waiting for me to wake up so we can smile at each other. And every time I make space and pause to listen in prayer, I learn again to open my eyes and see Him there. Waiting for me. Big goofy grin on His face.

What about you? Did anyone ever teach you to pause, to hold the phone and encounter God, with or without words? Would you like to practice now?

If you were to pause and imagine holding your heart out to Jesus, what would your heart look like? What would it feel like? Can you see it? Ask Jesus what He sees, and anything He would want you to notice about your heart today.

Or what would it be like to imagine waking up from a deep sleep, seeing God looking at you with affection? Make space and let yourself soak in the warmth of that reality for a moment. Is there anything you want to say to Him? Is there anything He's been waiting to say to you?

God of all Creation, I choose to believe You can and will communicate with me. You created me to be in relationship with You, and I long to encounter you everywhere: in the pages of Scripture, in the gift of my imagination, in the everyday moments of my listening life. Help me grow to hear and see You speaking in all things. Thank you for receiving my heart. Thank you for being patient to wait for me to wake up. Thank you for smiling at me. Amen.

Chapter 32

Promiscuous Creativity meets Generous Community
by Christopher Greco

Christopher Greco is a US-based theatre artist, educator, and pastor. He led worship and helped devise "out of the box" expressive activities at Journey training conferences.

We live in a New England wood. Pine trees and pine cones are everywhere. I take comfort in crunching along a path of these symbolic life-bearers because they are prickly, like me, and they are wastefully generative. A single tree drops an excessive volume of cones, each designed to protect excessive numbers of tiny seeds that live on for years and may never result in another pine tree. It's downright masturbatory.

I would know. My history of sexualized addiction began in childhood when primal insecurities about my maleness fused with my propensity for grandiose dreams of fame and fortune and a shot of pubescent testosterone. Of course, I didn't have these insights and words at the time—good thing, too, because it would have made it even harder to converse with male peers who were already stumped by my quick words and witty observations. I am embarrassed to admit I tried to make friends by quoting Monty Python as a 12-year-old. It didn't work. My peculiar path to manhood was a rollercoaster through perpetual loops of longing and perennial disappointment, isolation, and self-hatred. Would that somebody might have entered the scene to counsel me and spare me from 15 years of compulsive shame-inducing private behaviour. Although, I probably wouldn't have listened to them.

Emergent adulthood required prayerful bushwhacking through question-begging, soul-wrestling, relationship-wringing hyperbole to discover what I really felt about myself and other people and why. And what's God got to do with any of it? Exhaustedly and unexpectedly, I entered a first period of sobriety from sex with self in my mid-20's, several months before I was to be married. I'm grateful for this undeserved grace that made stillness and actual companionship possible for the first time in my life.

From year one, my married life has been satisfying, personally and mutually fruitful, and mostly free of the angst of my self-discovery years. My deep fear of being unlovable has been daily cleansed and bandaged by a woman who has uncovered for me, over years, a grave conviction that lurked deeper still: maybe I am incapable of loving another. Fear was proved wrong on both sides of love. The give and take and push and pull of love received and love given, over days and years, is a once-in-a-lifetime-is-enough private miracle between my wife and me. We are the only ones that truly apprehend the privilege we stumbled into and haven't lost 30 years later. Perhaps that's how it should be.

One problem in addiction is that we take symbolic things literally, and we act on them urgently. A corollary problem in addiction recovery is that we stay literal, and we think the problem we have is with sex or booze or food and now it's time to be tame and well-behaved. Avoiding temptation is a must early on, but eventually, we must befriend, suffer, confront, and decode what tempts us in order to freely choose something better. Our addiction is evidence that we habitually misinterpret our own feelings and squander our creativity when faced with floods of anxiety and pain. An easy to overlook ingredient of my journey out of masturbatory hell was the very thing that kicked it off: a fervent and fanciful imagination coping with chaotic helplessness. In a word, wildness. As the pine cone attests, effusive creativity is our imprimatur (approval and sanction) as *Imago Dei*, and so we must reclaim and repurpose the very energies that propelled us into addiction rather than just say no to them. And we must do so in the presence of other people.

My getting sober coincided with writing angry plays, composing desperate songs, and learning how to sustain non-sexualized intimacy with men and with women of all ages. The playwright trope of becoming dissolute, oversexed, and alcoholic in order to express my personal truth is the opposite of what I needed. I didn't need to lose myself in cliche sex, drugs, and rock and roll to become a true artist; I had already done that imaginatively. I needed to find myself as a whole and reliable friend and partner and father in the world of flesh and blood humans, and to keep creating. What I found with my wife and sons, and what I found in my periodic stints with the community of Journey Canada, was wholesome, sustainable, and extravagant wildness. We didn't dance in the dark of the pulsing nightclub but rather danced in the light of morning while singing songs about Jesus amidst flying fabric and liturgical fusion. (Should I be embarrassed?)

Our intersection with Journey Canada began early in our marriage, igniting in us the possibility of having company as we pursued an artistic, individuated Jesus-rooted spirituality. I found my West Canadian comrades to be less competitive, less conforming, more collaborative, and more aesthetically wild and free than their red-white-and-blue counterparts. They seemed not to be offended by my idiosyncrasies but to be inspired by them.

I grew up in a world where males were unsafe, predatory, self-deceived, and other-deceiving. Uncreative and oversexed, dangerous and mostly unreachable. Females appeared as mirages in the desert wasteland. Emotionally intelligent, superior, overreaching, subtly manipulative, unpredictably available and unavailable as I moved toward them. Only men who carried cowboy swagger, as I most certainly did not, won the day and seemed to truly capture the hearts of the women (and men) I knew.

South of the border in the triumphal and rigid home of the brave, it has been easy for me to conclude that I have to choose between Marlboro masculinity or pastel femininity, winning or losing, between authenticity or community, between being an artist or a Christian minister. The friends my wife and I met through Journey Canada testified to a both-and paradigm with a wider dynamic range, or what the German poet Rilke embraced as suffering with laughter.[62]

While my early adult Christian circles brought me into relationship with men and women who defied these internalized (and admittedly harsh) judgments and stereotypes, I have found American Christianity can be neutralized by unconscious cultural resistance to depth, honesty, and anything that doesn't sell and smile. Our individuality as men and women is undermined over time by such lack of range and reflection, and thus our relationships and our expression of sexuality and spirituality can languish in two-dimensionality. To name this within Christian churches is often to sever fellowship because it is perceived as harsh and judgmental (however accurate). My interactions with men and women in and around the Journey Canada team revealed that it's possible to embody multidimensional masculinity and femininity in community without being overruled or undermined by other people's baggage, expectations, and backlash—theological, political, or otherwise.

We are wise to take a lesson from the pine trees to root ourselves in one locale and keep improvising and innovating. We're going to produce lots of unnecessary ideas, initiatives, and even feelings. Many will be unknowingly trampled underfoot. If we are around

---

[62] Rainer Maria Rilke, Anita Barrows, and Joanna Rogers Macy, *Rilke's Book of Hours: Love Poems to God* (2005).

people who disapprove of our extravagant outpouring because they find us confounding—or theologically suspect—we're not in the right woods. When I recall my Journey Canada experiences, I see glimpses of faith without pretense, truth telling without superiority, aesthetics without perfectionism, common action without uniformity, difference without threat, wisdom without formula, passion amidst uncertainty. This is what I think it means to be *Christ*-ian.

I am grateful for Journey Canada's capacity to marry creativity and personal integrity where the Living God is allowed to be a wild and free Other who refuses to lead us along predictable and commodifiable paths. This God compassionately views our excessive pine cone production as a reflection of His own glorious creativity, even when it is sometimes sullied by our addictive tendencies. Nothing that a sprinkle of grace can't cover over and redeem. I wish my day-to-day life had more intersections with brothers and sisters like these. Because of the rareness and value of their particular flavor of creative spiritual community, how much more is their impact felt every day of my life in a New England wood.

Chapter 33

A Simple Practice for a Life of Prayer
by Kathryn Alarie

Kathryn Alarie is a Montreal based counsellor, spiritual director, and speaker. She is a former long-term Journey Quebec coordinator.

"Help me Jesus!" is one of my favorite prayers. Sometimes, I succinctly shorten this prayer to, "Jesus... Jesus... Jesus." His beautiful name means to rescue, save, or deliver. So, every time I repeat or speak out the name of Jesus, I am asking Him to save or help me, which is a powerful and effective arrow prayer.

"Arrow" prayers are quick, short, simple prayers that direct our thoughts and lift our souls to God. Arrows can conjure up images of weapons, hitting the target or piercing the darkness or the heavens. We often instinctively use them in emergencies or tense situations, when we need immediate help, strength or inspiration. So, when we are feeling anxious, threatened or tempted, we may simply pray, "Lord Jesus, have mercy on me" or "Lord strengthen me now," or "Please Lord let no evil befall me."

Have you ever found yourself driving by a road accident and asking God to protect and heal or bless the people involved in the scene? If so, you are offering up an arrow prayer. Arrow or "bullet" prayers can be used anywhere or anytime—before an exam or meeting, waiting for the subway or in a grocery line— times when we can't stop to sit down or contemplate for too long.

Some examples of quick, one-phrase prayers are:
"You alone are God and there is no other."
"Glory be to the Father, to the Son, and to the Holy Spirit."
"I am your beloved and you are mine."
"Thank-you God for your loving kindness, that is better than life."
"O Lord, I believe but help my unbelief."
"O my God, please make haste to help me..."

Frank Laubach coined the term flash prayers, developing the idea of praying short intercessory prayers for people we meet or see in our day-to-day activities. For example, if you see someone walking down the street, you may pray for them that the joy of the Lord or an awareness of His presence would spring up in them. Or if you are riding the subway or the bus, you might invite Jesus to walk up and down the aisles and speak words of blessing over everyone. Laubach and others, who have consistently prayed flash prayers, have noted that while some people reveal no response, others look up and smile. Occasionally, the whole atmosphere changes. It makes for an interesting experiment in prayer and undoubtedly helps us capture or tune in to God's heart for others.

Short, arrow prayers are a means of grace by which we can intercede for others, petition for ourselves, or simply thank God for His goodness. In my own journey of faith, even after 35 years of walking with Jesus, I still struggle, at times, with shame, anxiety, and the tyranny of not being good enough. To counter this, I regularly send out an arrow prayer, repeating to myself that, "I am in Him and He is enough. I have you Lord, I have enough." This reminds me of God's words to Paul when He said, "My grace is sufficient for you."[63] Other times, when I feel particularly anxious, I stop and repeat, "Sweet peace of the Prince of Peace, calm and quiet my soul" and I allow Him to enfold me in His presence.

---

[63] 2 Cor. 12:9

Another time when I tend to pray short quick prayers is on my daily hour-long walks. Generally, I don't use this time to fervently intercede for others but to simply enjoy His presence, finding God in all things. If I see a robin or a red cardinal, a budding flower, or a snow-covered pine, I pause and thank God for His glorious creation. When I reach the top of a particular hill, I stop and ask Jesus for His blessing of health, safety, empowering, or infilling for whoever I have on my mind.

Some people may be skeptical or critical of short prayers, reasoning that they are too easy, a bit frivolous, or a short-cut and that we need to be more focused and devoted in our communion with God. Indeed arrow prayers are not meant to replace other forms of prayer but to complement them. We are exhorted to pray without ceasing.[64] Might short prayers be one way of entering into a continual attitude of prayer? Of course, prayer is more than speaking; it involves the important element of also listening to God. I would hope that for myself and others that our short prayers would be flowing out of an ongoing, deeper union with Him.

Consider the story of Nehemiah. Some people believe that Nehemiah, the cupbearer to the king of Persia, prayed an arrow prayer when the king asked why he was sad and what he needed. In Nehemiah 2:4b, it reads, "So I (Nehemiah) prayed to the God of Heaven" and then he immediately explained to King Artaxerxes his request. However, prior to this encounter and opportune moment, Nehemiah had been interceding fervently for some days, confessing and asking God for favor and mercy on his people Israel.

Whether we are praying short or long prayers, what is central is to try and understand the heart of God, so that we may pray in accordance with His desire and will. Jesus is always our greatest

---

[64] 1 Thess. 5:17

example and model in how to pray. He spent much time alone, communing with His Father, even and perhaps especially in the midst of His busy days of ministering and teaching. Yet, He also offered up arrow prayers to His Father; for example, just before He raised Lazarus from the dead and before He fed the 5000.[65] Because Jesus often talked and listened to His Father for longer periods, when a specific situation came up, He already knew what to pray.

In my own life, just before I am scheduled to counsel, teach, or serve in some manner, I almost always pray a short prayer like, "Lord, I trust that showing up in faith is enough. Thank-you Holy Spirit that you are here with me." Oftentimes I add, "I may not be able to do everything but I can do something, together with you. You are the great counsellor or teacher. Guide me in your wisdom and give me your love and compassion for this person or group." Later, once I am in a counselling or small group session, I often pray inwardly, "Lord, what are you doing here? Or what do you want me to do?" Sometimes, I do not hear well but most often the Holy Spirit does intervene and provides the direction, comfort, or affirmation needed.

Prayer, short or long, is the ultimate way to communicate with God and it can lead us directly to His heart. It can also be the very channel by which we receive supernatural strength and power, allowing us to richly bless others, as well as ourselves. As Cynthia Lewis said, "If your day is hemmed in with prayer, it is less likely to become unravelled."[66]

---

[65] John 11:41, Matt. 14:19

[66] Crosswalk Editorial Staff, "40+ Prayer Quotes for Daily Inspiration and Powerful Encouragement," Crosswalk.com https://www.crosswalk. com/faith/spiritual-life/inspiring-quotes/31-prayer-quotes-be-inspired-and-encouraged.html.

Chapter 34

Using Borrowed Words in Prayer
by Arabella Cheng

Arabella Cheng works as Journey's ministry development coordinator and lives in Vancouver. In addition to writing, she loves burgers, spreadsheets and hiking.

"I think you have shingles," the doctor said, examining the rash that ran up my arm as I described the discomfort in my neck and shoulders which had worsened into the screaming pain I now felt. Unfortunately, I had missed the window when antivirals would have been most effective, so I was now in for three weeks of agonizing and debilitating pain, lots of meds, and disturbed sleep. Worse yet, shingles hit while I was reeling from some heavy situations that had pushed me into a morass of disorientation and weariness.

Amid this desolation, I began to discover an upholding gift in the Daily Office—the ancient practice of morning, midday, and evening prayers. The Offices originated in the monastic communities of the early Christian centuries and are practiced in Anglican and Catholic traditions. Services of morning and evening prayer, they incorporate Psalms and other readings of Scripture, the Lord's Prayer, collects (short, set prayers), confession, thanksgiving, petition, and benediction.

Earlier in the year, a few months into the COVID-19 pandemic, I had started practicing the Daily Office—not every morning and evening, but regularly enough that I was forming a habit of prayer and solitude. And so, the evening I was diagnosed, I prayed the Office as I went to bed. Continuing the cycle of morning and evening prayers those terrible weeks steadied me and brought the light and comfort of Christ into my darkness and distress.

It has been a slow nine-month recovery, happening during the pandemic, together with waves of difficult events and losses that have brought fear, bewilderment, anger, discouragement, and sorrow. Through all the turmoil, this spiritual practice has accompanied, anchored, and even transformed me through the struggle and hardship as I've been led to lean into Jesus. As I practice this ancient pattern of prayer, I am discovering what a sustaining gift it can be.

The Gift of Framing

The Daily Office, also called the Liturgy of the Hours, creates a frame for the day. Just as the framing of a building gives it shape and support, the Office frames the hours in my day, setting the tone or rhythm. It's not another item to fit into my list of obligations, rather, setting aside sacred times for prayer and to be with God at the beginning and end of the day (and throughout) is a way to order life. Monastic communities centre all of life's activities around these prayers; they are the fundamental rhythm of their communal life. I see this kind of ordering in Jesus' life in His setting aside times of solitude to be with His Father: "Very early in the morning, while it was still dark, Jesus got up, left the house and went off to a solitary place, where he prayed."[67] I imagine these were times of praying the Psalms and nurturing His intimate connection with His Father, which prepared and enabled Jesus to do His Father's work in the world.

This practice also helps frame how I live out my day as I proclaim and affirm who God is—good, faithful, personal, powerful, at

---

[67] Mark 1:35 NIV

work in our world, restoring all creation to Himself. As I pray, I find myself in the presence of the Creator of the universe and my Source of life; He reminds me that He is God, and I am not. He invites me to rejoice in each day as a gift, to respond with praise and thanks, to commit myself, waking and sleeping, to Him, to know that I am held, whether in joy or sorrow.

When pain and helplessness gripped me, these regular times of prayer reminded me that God sees and holds me and my days. He hears and responds to my cries. He is my trustworthy Good Shepherd who provides for me. I was awakened to the reality of Jesus' presence, grace, and closeness—that He is the suffering Christ who intimately knows my pain and darkness and brings consolation beyond understanding.

The Gift of Words

The set words and structure are another gift of the Daily Office. I grew up in the Anglican tradition, praying the same prayers Sunday after Sunday. Being a "good girl," I followed along dutifully. I memorized the words and "knew" them, the way I knew about God, with my mind but not my heart. As my spiritual journey progressed, I came to know God more personally, and He started reconnecting my head and heart. I dismissed this way of prayer and explored praying extemporaneously and with my imagination. But eventually, I sensed an invitation back to the prayers of my childhood.

Approaching these prayers as a more whole person has opened me up to discover them anew. I now pray the words from a deeper place—engaging my head, my heart, my body, and even my imagination. When I contemplate the words of the Office, I'm struck by how beautifully and thoughtfully they have been written and arranged and how Scripture saturates them. I am aware of their depth, richness and meaning; they describe the reality of our triune God and lead me into that reality.

I realize too, that those words I prayed all those childhood Sundays were not senseless repetition; rather, they have shaped me and my spirituality and deepened in me the truth of God's character. As I "go through the motions" and pray the words with my heart, mind, and soul each day, I discover the gift in the words, and they form me. In the Offices I follow, I begin each morning with Psalm 63:1 (NIV): "You, God, are my God, earnestly I seek you; I thirst for you, my whole being longs for you..." Praying this day after day, week after week, has done something in me. I am reminded that whatever the day may bring, God is God, He is my God, and I am His. I am being awakened to my deepest yearning, which is for God Himself; only He can quench my soul's thirst and so I am led to seek Him all the more.

Yet another gift of these set prayers is that they are, simply, there— for me to pray when I don't know how to pray. During this shingles journey, I had times of overwhelming pain, mind fog, and slowness. Words and thoughts were often elusive and out of my grasp, or I just didn't have anything in me to pray. It was reassuring to have the words there before me. They made a way for me to articulate the truths about God, even when I wasn't sure of them or didn't feel it. They gave voice to the wordless cries of my heart and taught me how to pray.

The Gift of Connection
Lastly, through the Daily Office I have experienced the gift of connection—to God, myself, and others.

This spiritual practice makes a way to abide in Jesus as He abides in me; it assures me of His certain presence with me. It continually points me to Father, Son, and Spirit, in whom I find my true home; Jesus draws me deeper into His life, where I come to know more of who He is and more of who I am. In the time and space I dedicate to fixing my eyes on Him and being aware of His loving gaze upon me, I enter into the truth that He is my Heavenly Father and I am His beloved daughter, fully loved, known, and seen. How precious it has been to begin and end my days "Know[ing] that the Lord is God. It is He that has made us, and we are His; we are His people and the sheep of His pasture."[68]

In the Office I also connect with myself as it makes space for me to be more attentive to my inner life and emotions and to articulate the depths of my heart, largely through praying the Psalms. On days when I am in pain, the Psalms express the cries of my heart to the Lord and my trust in Him. Other days, they connect and give voice to my deeper thoughts, feelings, and longings.

Finally, the Office connects me to the body of Christ. As the "we" and "us" language of the Office indicates, it can be prayed in community. Whether I pray in community or in solitude, I pray neither alone nor privately, for these words wonderfully remind me that I am part of a larger family, united in one body by the one Spirit. How profound and encouraging it is to be praying words that countless Christians throughout the ages have prayed, and to join in prayer with brothers and sisters all around the world today!

The prayers of intercession prompt me to turn my attention beyond myself towards the needs of others in the Church and the world. During my recovery, I was limited in what I could do for others physically or practically, but through the Office, I found that I could pray for them. I noticed a growing stirring to pray for others as the Spirit brought them to mind.

As I continue to practice the Daily Office, the Spirit of Christ is slowly shaping me as I receive the gifts of framing, words, and connection. Some days I find it a struggle, yet choose to do it, and other days I let it go, but I am seeing the fruit of consistency over time. I enjoy and practice other ways of praying, but I am finding treasure in beginning with and returning to the Office.

---

[68] Ps. 100:3 NIV

The pandemic of this last year has brought much sorrow, uncertainty, disconnection, waiting, and disappointment to our individual and collective lives. Many of us and our families experienced additional difficulties and many other world events were deeply unsettling and troubling. In the inevitable messiness, chaos, and brokenness we face, the Daily Office provides a pathway and light through the darkness, suffering, injustice, and loss in our world.

The Office can be a sustaining, steadying, anchoring practice because it leads us into the presence of our triune God who remains present with us, faithful and good, bringing hope, and making all things new. He draws us into His divine life and purpose and strengthens us to live as His followers in our world, seeing through His eyes and knowing His heart. The Daily Office has been for me, as for so many disciples through the ages and around the world, a door into the transformation and the deeper life with Him He invites us to.

Chapter 35

Fear is Replaced by Love
by Scott Neufeld

Scott Neufeld has been on staff with Journey Canada since 2015 and loves cooking, swimming, his wife and his new daughter. He just moved to Southern Ontario from the Lower Mainland, BC and works as Journey's resource facilitator and the West-of-Toronto program coordinator.

For years if I got silent, it was anything *but* silent. A cacophony of unpleasant voices would surface. Voices of shame, anxiety, fear, insecurity, and pain would grow in the stillness. I am still wary of silence. Even now, on the other side of spelunking with the Lord into the darkest places of my heart, and having come to know His kindness, friendship and love; even still I am hesitant to sit with Him in silence. What will the silence reveal? What will the voices say?

And yet right in the midst of the uncertainty is the invitation from Christ to be still *with Him*. To wait long enough to hear His voice underneath the other voices, calling me into being, calling me into love. It took me many years to find the courage and discipline to be silent long enough to hear and give voice to the deepest cries of my heart.

I grew up in a mid-size town referred to as the Bible Belt of British Columbia. The Lord gave me a sensitive soul—I feel life deeply— and to this day I have to wrestle with not allowing my feelings to dictate my reality. As a child I found it difficult to navigate negative feelings like anger and sadness so I learned to bottle them up. I've found that it is in silence that the buried feelings of my heart tend to reveal themselves. This is why I fled from silence—why I would lose myself in novels as a boy, then computer games, then pornography—to fill the silence with noise, with *anything*.

Silence was an invitation for my heart to speak, and I did not want to hear what my heart had to say! I knew my heart had dark things hidden inside and I wanted to avoid becoming acquainted with that darkness at all costs. Exploring my heart felt like heading down into a labyrinthine mine without a flashlight. *No, thank you.* So, I retreated onto the surface, playing games, staying distracted, staying numb. This suited me throughout my childhood, and my coping behaviours were a welcome part of getting through.

I remember when I was 17 years old standing in the lobby of my high school talking with some friends about our weekend plans, and a friend said she was going to "hang out with God" that evening at home. She told us how when she was really sad, she would speak with Him, and feel His presence with her in her room, comforting her. I looked at her with what must have been a very sceptical expression, "You're going to *hang out* with God?"

I had been a believer ever since I prayed to receive Jesus at five years old. I had attended church every Sunday my entire life, and I had never heard of someone having a personal relationship with Jesus. I was intrigued. This friend invited me and some friends to her youth group at a charismatic church. I had grown up in a Mennonite church, and this was in the 90s when most of the congregation was a sea of white hair, they had trombones in the church band, and where people who raised their hands to worship were considered ultra-spiritual in the best case, and completely out of their gourd in the worst case.

When I got to the youth service, the preacher was preaching with a passion I had never seen. My peers were falling to the ground right and left, people were dancing and it was all very foreign, and yet I could not deny the tangible experience of the presence of Jesus. For the first time in my life, I really felt Him in the atmosphere, and it was thick and warm and good. I sat down on one of the orange-carpeted pews, put my head in my hands and prayed, "Lord, I know there is more to you than I know. Show me the more."

This was the beginning of His invitation to go down into my very own Mines of Moria, where goblins and Balrogs lurked; into my heart. Into silence. That was 2003. In His slow and patient way, Jesus waited for me, inviting me to know myself, and to know Him. Paul says Christ dwells in our hearts,[69] it's where He makes His home in us, and I believe we must know our hearts if we are to visit with Him there. However, I spent the next nine years continuing to avoid, continuing to numb, continuing to fear silence and the voices that silence allowed to speak. I spent those years growing in my knowledge and love of the Lord, but I would not allow the Lord to take me very deep. It was a slow and painful education that eventually led me to desperation, and in 2012 I applied to the Journey Discipleship Course in Vancouver.

In my Journey small group, I was lowered through the ceiling to Jesus' feet week after week.[70] I was debilitated by shame and guilt and couldn't get to Jesus on my own. I was terrified of what He might speak into the silence if I *really* listened, if I opened my heart to Him. What if He said the thing that I had been fearing my entire life, that I was unlovable, that He was ashamed of me?

I had never prayed such honest prayers before Journey. I didn't know I had permission to pray what I really felt. My leaders gave me permission to be *real* with the *real God*. I spoke to Jesus, "Lord, I don't hate pornography. The truth is, I love it. And I also love you, will you help me? I don't think I can go on any further. Lord,

---

[69] Eph. 3:17

[70] Luke 5:17-39

I am so tangled up in my sin, please help me." I remember a leader asking me to imagine Jesus approaching me, but I would not let Him get too close. And when I told Jesus to "stop," He did. He respected me and my boundaries. This helped my heart to open more. I let Him take one more step. As the weeks progressed the silence became less terrifying. The Lord had lit a torch and was offering to walk *with me* into the recesses of my heart. As I waited in the stillness, His voice was becoming louder and clearer than the voices of shame, anxiety, and fear.

When I stopped filling the space with words, it gave the Lord the opportunity to fill my heart, and my heart began to surrender as a response to the beauty and joy He was showing me. I prayed, "If this is Jesus, the most loving, tender, and compassionate man I've ever met, then I give him my whole heart." I remember seeing a picture in prayer near the end of the course of Jesus' nail-scarred hand extended to me in an invitation of discipleship. I took it, and together we ventured down, down, down into the darkness. Jesus began to shed His love abroad in my heart.[71]

At home, I began to cultivate times of silence, but now I was allowing Jesus to take me places I didn't want to go. As I allowed the heat of the Lord's loving gaze on my heart, the dross would rise to the surface. The voices of anxiety and shame were given full voice, and I would share what they said to Jesus; in the presence of my Best Friend. Then Jesus would share what He wanted to say to me, and His words of love, affirmation, acceptance, and kindness were like a balm. I've heard it said that when we allow the Lord's love to come into our hearts, it will push pain out, like a spiritual law of displacement.

I was experiencing this in my quiet times with the Lord; a profound healing was happening on the one hand, and a release of deep pain on the other. Sometimes I would collapse to the floor as years of

---

[71] Romans 5:5

repressed pain were released to Jesus and the cross. Sometimes it felt like Mount Vesuvius was erupting and other days it was slow, like molasses. What mattered was He was with me, and I knew it now. Silence alone is isolation; silence with a good friend is healing. I was discovering in the stillness that beyond the fear of darkness lay a friendship with Jesus. Henri Nouwen touched on this when he said:

> But if we have the discipline to stay put and not let these dark voices intimidate us, they will gradually lose their strength and recede into the background, creating space for the softer, gentler voices of the light... They have been speaking to us since before we were born, and they reveal to us that there is no darkness in the One who sent us into the world, only light. They are part of God's voice calling us from all eternity: "My beloved child, my favorite one, my joy."[72]

Lately the Lord's been reminding me to pray that He would strengthen me to meet Him in that sacred quiet space. Entering silence with the Maker of Heaven and Earth takes courage because it is vulnerable and can be uncomfortable, and yet as I've chosen to stay, I've found friendship with the Prince of Peace.

---

[72] Henri Nouwen, *Can You Drink the Cup?* (2006).

Chapter 36

Places that may not be Places
by Amy Donaldson

*A*my Donaldson is the development coordinator for Journey Asia. She finds great joy in the silence of creation with the best vantage point from her kayak.

I feel the airplane bank then straighten for its final descent. I enjoy the window seat, especially on a clear day where I can see the skyscrapers stacked up on one another huddled around Victoria Harbour. I focus on all the tiny islands spotting the South China Sea, and peace washes over me as I see my island out there amongst the many.

Clearing my final obstacle—immigration and customs—my pace picks up as my pilgrimage begins. I feel more alive as I take the train into the heart of Hong Kong, a compact country of over seven million people.

The weight of ministry and the wear and tear of my Asian travels begin to fall away. I make a quick exit off the train to catch a slow ferry, sitting on the upper deck taking in the harbour views with the saltwater breeze washing over me, waking me up for what lies ahead. I exit my ferry at Cheung Chau Island and hike into the heart of the fishing village, around the beach, and up, up, up to the Christian guest house. I breathe in my surroundings of lush tropical trees and flowers, birds singing, butterflies flitting from leaf to petal, and frogs jumping off the path. This portion of the island was set aside by the British government for churches: the Anglican's prayer house, the Catholic's sprawling retreat center, the Salvation Army's youth camp, the Alliance's seminary. To me, it is a place I intentionally retreat to twice a year. Early in the morning and late each evening, I make the two-minute trek to any of the large rock cliffs overlooking the sea. I enter the silence knowing I will encounter God. This is my Thin Place.

Christians throughout history have identified that there are some actual physical locations where one can more readily connect with God; this is considered a thin place. These are sacred places where it seems as if the space between the Divine and the created is narrower. Here the "veil" that separates the spiritual realm and the earthly world is "thin" or especially porous such that God is believed to "leak through" more easily.[73]

The idea of thin places was new to me and as I read more, I discovered this idea connected to Celtic Spirituality which believes there are particular locations such as Iona in Scotland where the Divine touches us more easily. Another example might be found by those who set out on pilgrimage to walk the Camino de Santiago ending at the Cathedral of Santiago de Compostela in Spain. Often our sense of the sacred is more pronounced, heaven touching us, in places like a chapel, church, or monastery where there have been centuries of prayers spoken.

I talked to my Spiritual Director about this concept and she encouraged me to read through my prayer journals and watch for my own thin places. I discovered the island of Cheung Chau as a place where I more easily encountered my Creator and often took pilgrimage there. I also realized God's generous provision of a new thin place as Hong Kong became less accessible due to unrest and COVID-19. These past three years, I have retreated to an Ignatian center in the US where I anticipate a more porous, sacred space.

---

[73] William Barry, *Friendship Like No Other* (2009).

Pause and reflect on your own spiritual journey; is there a particular location where you have experienced a thin place?

I wondered if a thin place had to be a particular location at all. I see the Divine One encountering me in moments, not just physical locations. I considered God's creation as a thin space for me, such as a male cardinal in all his brilliant red beauty. This bird has always had a special place in my heart as it symbolizes a safe, generous love. One of my favorite times as a child was sitting at my grandpa's breakfast table. Each morning he would put a peanut on the windowsill and then whistle. His cardinal, affectionately named Pedro, would land and chirp at him. I felt my grandpa's affection and attention as he shared with me his bond with the little red bird.

Fast forward forty years: I am on retreat and I have been wrestling for days with deep-seated lies about God and me which were laid like a concrete foundation through my childhood sexual abuse. After days of questioning, arguing, jackhammering, and crying out, His Love finally broke my heart. I was undone.

I could see intimate Love, Jesus Himself, encompassing, cocooning me in love even amid heinous abuse. I believed Him. As I got up off the floor of that little chapel in the woods, I moved to the porch to sit, to breathe as I looked out on the river winding through the trees. And then it happened!

With my heart's home surrounded by love, yet lingering lies licking at the edges of my heart, a male cardinal landed on a branch just yards away. He did not flit from branch to branch. No, he faced me full on and sang loudly to me for over ten minutes. I heard God say through this Love song, "Amy, I see you! Even in the worst moments of your life, I was with you. I AM with you. I love you!" There was no twisting and turning away from this encounter with a personal God who knew my heart language.

Might the cardinal be my thin space? Throughout the remainder of the retreat, I was bombarded by red birds to the point of being comical. How could I forget His immense, encompassing love? One landing on my bedroom windowsill looking in at me. Cardinals buzzing by my head as I walked in the woods. Another hopping on the rocks as I sat down by the creek. Divine Love, touching the earth, meeting me in this thin space. Now, wherever I am, when a male cardinal comes into view, I anticipate an encounter with God.

I believe we can experience the Divine breaking into our ordinary lives in a given moment, not only through His creation as in a red bird or in the sun setting over the sea's horizon, but maybe as we hold our newborn baby or as we take in the beauty of a piece of art or as we have an intimate conversation with a dear friend or as we recite with many other voices that familiar century-worn liturgy or as we sit with a dying loved one who is completing their earthly journey.

Pause and consider where you have experienced a moment of thin space.

I wonder if we can actively create an environment that cultivates a thin space? I know, God is the One who moves heaven to earth, but can we position ourselves? I like the chapter right before this one as I believe there is a relationship between silence and thin spaces. I have often missed the Divine encounter due to all my internal noises (my to-do list, the lies bombarding me, my addictions) as well as my external noises (traffic, text messages vibrating, work pressures). As I choose to come into external and internal silence, I can come present to not only myself but also to God.

As we turn our attention, tuning into the Divine, anticipating... Might not heaven come and touch earth? Possibly, intimately touching us? But are we quiet enough to even realize it? "Silence is not to be shunned as empty space, but to be befriended as fertile ground for intimacy with God."[74]

I am grateful for the ministry of Journey that has helped me grow the quiet internal space by battling lies, self-hatred, and shame left from abuse, betrayals, and my addictions. Journey was the first place I realized Jesus wanted to talk to me. He desired all of me to "draw near to Him, to incline my ear to listen, so my soul would live" (Isaiah 55:3). It became safe to come into silence and listen. We now have a conversational relationship that allows me to dwell with Him in my heart's home.

Pause and reflect on how you might begin creating external and internal silence.

As you consider your journey, reflect not only on if you have experienced thin spaces but how you might cultivate them in your walk with God. I intentionally set aside time and money for retreats to my thin place. It doesn't have to be across the ocean or even a prayer chapel in the woods; it can be on your back patio or even in a chair in your apartment. Choose internal silence. Come present to God and visit your thin place often.

I just returned from an eight-day retreat to my thin place, and I saw myself getting more focused on the places of past connection, as if I could control the encounter. Maybe if I go back to that spot, I can open the door to an encounter with Him this time. I could see Him smiling as He challenged me, "Amy, this is a real relationship, remember? You can't control this."

Once acknowledged, name your thin spaces then guard them. They are sacred. I do not just invite anyone into my heart cathedral or even my external cathedrals. This is where I dwell freely communing with my Beloved, and it is a holy place that is

---

[74] Thomas Ashbrook, *Mansions of the Heart* (2009).

to be set apart. My friend, fiercely protect them. Even consider keeping your devices (the internet, the outside world, texts, emails) and the things that distract you out of your sacred spaces.

Pause and consider ways you can participate with God in cultivating your thin spaces.

As I reflect on these thin spaces, my heart specifically turns to Jesus. Where do I see Him, the Incarnate One, and thin places meeting? My mind immediately jumps to His baptism; Jesus submerged in the waters of our earthly planet then kissed with the Father's audible blessing.[75] And then I recall His death which tore the veil in the temple that separated God from us.[76] I realize that in Jesus, we can unabashedly come face to face with God.

Isn't Jesus the Place where the Divine and the created meet?[77] He is the Son of God and the Son of Man who came and walked with us. When we see Jesus, we see God our Loving Father. When I contemplate this reality, my response is, could there be any thinner place than Jesus? And then I remember His promise, the Spirit of Christ indwells us. As I encounter Him in my innermost being, my spirit in union with His Spirit, I pause and wonder; if Jesus who is The Divine Place indwells me the created, then could I not be a Thin Place?

---

[75] Matt. 3:13-17

[76] Luke 23:44-46

[77] William Barry, *Friendship Like No Other* (2009).

Made in the USA
Coppell, TX
14 April 2022

76178072R00129